ROOTED
IN
GRACE

Finding What Strengthens Your Faith

Jesse Bradley

ISBN 978-1-105-51725-9

Dedication

To my sweet wife, Laurie. Where would I be without you? I'm so grateful for you and your prayers, insights, and time spent listening. To our wonderful children who inspire beyond words. To my sisters whom I laugh with often. And to my parents whom I love deeply and are so dear to me.

100% of the profits of this book are given to Compassion International® which is a Christian organization that releases children from poverty throughout the world.
www.compassion.com

Introduced to Grace

When I first experienced grace, it felt almost too good to be true. And yet it could not have been more real. I sincerely believed I was pursuing grace, but later realized that I was the one who was being pursued first. The faithfulness, kindness, and mercy of God can truly soften any heart, even a calloused heart like mine. God has so many ways of showering His grace, and His gifts are usually far deeper, richer, and more personal than I initially realized.

I never expected to become a follower of Jesus. Growing up, I was literally surrounded by churches in our neighborhood; but I wasn't interested, and they stayed away from me. The first time I read the Bible was for a college course, *Introduction to World Religions*, in my Freshman year at Dartmouth College. To my surprise, I discovered that the Bible was the most grace-filled book I had ever encountered, contemplated, or digested. By studying the Gospel of John, simply because it was part of my college class assignment, God changed my life and my perspective forever.

As I read the Bible, I was skeptical about Jesus and had many questions. How could I have a relationship with the living God? Could I rely on the truths spoken by a young Jewish carpenter who lived two thousand years ago? How real is heaven? At that time, my life looked successful on the outside: an Ivy League student with solid grades, a young man with many friends, a member of a championship soccer team, and a recipient of many personal awards. Yet deep inside, there was a void that puzzled me. Gradually, over the course of a year, I realized how much Jesus had done for me, and I became ready to follow Him. Grace is an undeserved gift. When I put my trust in Jesus, I received the gift of peace with God and eternal life, something I could never earn. It's a gift I have thoroughly enjoyed and continue to unwrap.

This book is born out of my life experiences. After college, I took the opportunity to play professional soccer in Zimbabwe. I never dreamed of becoming a pastor. A near-death illness redirected my life in countless ways. As a result, there have been unexpected turns along my journey, and many of them are interwoven into this book. The grace of God is something I'm passionate about! I really want people to know how much they are loved by God. My prayer is that this book will help you experience the joy of Jesus, and that grace will become more real and more precious to you everyday.

Rooted In Grace

My hope is that *Rooted In Grace* will be spiritually refreshing. You can choose how to proceed through the various topics, reflections, and studies. For many years, I felt lost in a massive maze as I opened up the Bible and was unsure where to find specific verses and themes. This book is designed to walk you through a wide range of passages and contains portions of Scripture from all 66 books in the Bible. You will find insights and practical principles in God's Word. God's grace transforms you from the inside out and renews your mind.

This book will provide a helpful structure for your time spent with God. Each theme includes questions for your reflection. The "Deeper Study" section will guide you into a wide range of Bible passages that shed light on a specific topic. Each day concludes with a prayer that will support you in your communication with God.

In addition to reading the book yourself, another option is to read and discuss it with a friend, parent, child, or spouse. It can also become the material for a small group Bible study. Take what you gain from this book and share it with the people you love.

Contents

POWERFUL GRACE

God is glorified as He demonstrates His goodness and ability

1) ALL OF THIS IS YOURS

Passage: Ephesians 1:3-5

> *Praise be to the God and Father of our Lord Jesus Christ, who has blessed us in the heavenly realms with every spiritual blessing in Christ. For he chose us in him before the creation of the world to be holy and blameless in his sight. In love he predestined us to be adopted as his sons through Jesus Christ in accordance with his pleasure and will.*

Insight:

I received a surprise call one day that included an invitation to a sushi restaurant. Another couple invited my wife and me to dinner, and I was far more excited to spend time with them than I was to eat raw fish for the first time. With enough sauce, the sushi didn't taste as bad as I had imagined. The highlight of the night came later as the couple said goodbye to us. I asked how we would get home because we were at their house and they had picked us up. The man exclaimed, "With your car!" as he tossed me a set of keys to a Ford Mustang. I was speechless (and that doesn't happen very often). It was a gift—an incredible display of grace! They explained that someone had given them a car many years ago, and they wanted to repeat the gift. They even have a girl named Charis (which literally means grace). We did absolutely nothing to deserve the car, yet it was now ours. We were stunned in the best way; grace impacts your life as you realize how much you have been given.

To be the recipient of grace is extremely humbling. It is a combination of feeling unworthy and deeply appreciative. Accepting an unmerited gift from Jesus is part of drawing near to a Savior who grants us complete forgiveness and eternal pardon. It is possible to attend church for many years but never begin a relationship with God or receive His grace. In the passage above, the apostle Paul was writing to the church in Ephesus, explaining to them how much God has already given them. One of the most important spiritual steps as a Christian is realizing how much God loves you and how much Jesus has done for you.

Repentance simply means turning from rebellion against God and choosing to follow Jesus (it is a 180 degree U-turn and a new start). It happens when we are ready to put our trust in God, and even the ability to repent is a gift from Him. Receiving comes first, and then because of His kindness, we respond to God with worship and service. It is a bold statement when Paul says that God has given us every spiritual blessing and that we are blameless in God's sight through the sacrifice of Jesus. Take some time to read this section of Scripture, and throughout the day, think deeply about God's ability to uphold His grace in your life.

Application:

When someone decides to follow Jesus and puts his or her trust in Him, these are some of the blessings that are given to that person:

1) **Eternal Acceptance:** You have peace with God forever, and a life that will never end. You have been chosen and selected by God to dwell with Him forever in full pleasure and joy (Ephesians 1:1-5).

2) **Current Guidance:** God gives you wisdom when you ask Him for it in every situation. He will provide everything you

need, including the Holy Spirit, to spiritually thrive in any circumstance (Ephesians 1:3 and 1:8).

3) **Undeserved Benevolence:** There is nothing you could do to earn these gifts. You cannot boast that you have done it. He redeems you for His glory and your good (Ephesians 1:6-7).

4) **Constant Presence:** He will never leave you alone: the Holy Spirit is in you. Your best friend is right there with you all of the time. He literally resides inside you (Ephesians 1:9-13).

5) **Guaranteed Inheritance:** No one can take away God's gift, not even the devil can steal it. When God makes promises, He comes through (Ephesians 1:14).

Questions:

1) Which blessing stands out to you in Ephesians chapter one?

2) How would you describe these blessings in your own words?

3) Is it easy or difficult for you to receive big gifts from God?

4) Why does God treat us better than we deserve?

Deeper Study:

Romans 8:31-39. Nothing can separate you from the love of Christ.

Psalm 8. In all of God's vast creation, He specifically cares about you.

2 Samuel 22:1-51. It is good to remember what God has done for you.

Psalm 103. Praise God for His complete forgiveness and healing hand.

Zephaniah 3:14-17. God rejoices over you with singing.

Prayer:

Merciful God, thank You for paying the full price for my sins and rescuing me from spending eternity apart from You. It means so much to me to know that You accept me. I love You more than I love the gifts You give me. Please help me to realize what You have given me so that it will affect how I live everyday. I want to live in a way that brings You as much glory as possible. Please help me spread the good news about You to everyone. I pray this in Your name, Jesus. Amen.

2)   BECAUSE HE LIVES

Passage: 1 Corinthians 15:3-6

For what I received I passed on to you as of first importance: that Christ died for our sins according to the Scriptures, that he was buried, that he was raised on the third day according to the Scriptures, and that he appeared to Peter, and then to the Twelve. After that, he appeared to more than five hundred of the brothers at the same time...

Insight:

Losing a family member is one of the most difficult situations in life. Have you ever experienced this? I have led the funerals for two of my grandpas- one was a pioneer in the field of open-heart surgery and the other one was a paratrooper who fought in the Battle of The Bulge in World War II. I used to call one of my grandpas every Friday (which was my day off work) to talk and pray together. There are so many days when I miss my grandfathers and would just like to talk with them again. I admire my grandpas, and their deaths remind me that this life is not our full story. We can know where we are going after we die. It is not a false hope but a promise that is backed by solid evidence.

There are many things that are important in the Christian faith, but this is the most significant. We often hear the word "gospel," which literally means "good news," but we aren't sure what it means. The gospel is the heart and crux of Christianity. The good news has two sides: 1) Jesus died for your sins and 2) Jesus is alive, because He has risen from the grave. When you consider what Christ has done for us, His grace is overwhelming both on the cross and in His victory over death. His power over the grave has historical evidence, as there were many witnesses; and it also leaves us in awe of His supernatural power and grace.

Application:

Paul concludes, in 1 Corinthians chapter 15, that if Jesus is not risen: 1) Christianity is a lie, 2) your faith is worthless, 3) your loved ones can only perish, and 4) Christians are pathetic. In other words, our entire faith is on the line when it comes to the resurrection of Jesus.

Evidence:[1]

God has provided us with historical details that support the resurrection (1 Corinthians 15:5-8):

1) **Eyewitness reports:** There were over 500 people who actually saw the risen Lord!

2) **The disciples make a U-turn:** The disciples were discouraged and afraid until they saw Jesus alive again.

3) **The level of conviction:** Ten of the twelve original disciples were killed (John had a natural death and Judas killed himself). Would anyone ever die for a lie if they knew it wasn't true? The disciples were convinced because they experienced the risen Lord.

4) **The guarded tomb:** Roman soldiers were guarding Jesus' tomb and would be killed if they let anyone take His body. They made certain that no one was allowed to remove Jesus' body after burial.

5) **The empty tomb:** There is only one religious leader who overcame death, and He is not in the grave.

6) **The historical details:** In a male-dominated culture where, sadly, women were usually viewed as second-class citizens, women were the first to discover the risen Jesus. This encounter was from God.

7) **The rapid growth of the church:** In Jerusalem, the place where Jesus was seen alive again, the church exploded in size. About 3,000 people began to follow Jesus in one day (Acts 2:41).

Questions:

1) Why do you think people reject Jesus despite all of the evidence?
2) Which of the seven reasons above stands out to you the most?
3) Who can you share the evidence with this week?

Deeper Study:

John 20:1-31. Jesus wants people to look at the evidence of His resurrection.

John 11:17-44. Death was not and is not difficult for Jesus to overcome.

Revelation 1:4-8. Jesus is in Heaven now, but His return will be visible to all.

Acts 1:1-11. The gospel spreads through relationships.

Prayer:

Almighty God, even death can't stop You. Your plans prevail and Your love has been proven historically. Thank You for all of the clear evidence You have given for Your resurrection miracle. Thank You that our faith is supported by facts. Help me to spread the good news with courage and intelligence. In Jesus name I pray. Amen.

3)   NATURE SHOUTS GOD'S EXISTENCE

Passage: Proverbs 30:4

Who has gone up to heaven and come down? Who has gathered up the wind in the hollow of his hands? Who has wrapped up the waters in his cloak? Who has established all the ends of the earth? What is his name and the name of his son? Tell me if you know!

Insight:

Imagine this scene: you enter the heavenly courtroom and begin to ask questions. The first witness is the wind. You inquire, "Mr. Wind, who gathers you in the hollow of His hand?" And the second witness is the water. You ask, "Mr. Waters, who wraps you in His cloak?" And then the third witness: "Mrs. Earth, who established your domain?" Each answer is the same; it was God. God gives us multiple clues of His existence, both through creation and in His Word. This proverb is a series of questions because the author wants us to think about the strong hand behind the elements we observe.

Yes, God has given nature a practical purpose. The flowers of the field give pollen to bees and bring oxygen into the air (photosynthesis is no accident). But God also displays His creativity through the incredible variety, colors, and beauty of the same flowers. Like these flowers, nature is actively declaring the goodness and glory of God. It is an extension of His grace to us in a tangible way. When you spend time outside gardening, exercising, or traveling and you have that sense that God is with you and communicating through nature- don't ignore it. It's been my experience that some of the closest fellowship with God can happen while resting in awe underneath the sky or close to the ocean He created.

Application:

Romans 1:20 tells us that nature communicates two things very clearly: 1) God is real and 2) God is powerful. And because these truths are clearly seen in nature, humankind is now without excuse. We must acknowledge God as Creator. Colossians 1:16 tells us that all things were created by Jesus: in heaven and on earth, both visible and invisible. The ocean, the sunset, the mountains, the desert, the countless stars in the sky all remind us that we are to savor their beauty, and at the same time worship the One who made them.

Because He is truly gracious, God has revealed Himself in many ways: through the prophets, through the Bible, through our conscience, and through miracles. One of the most spectacular ways He has made Himself known is through nature. He wants us to see His creation so that we will be in awe of Him! If you are studying His creation or just walking along the beach, take time to appreciate what God has made for His glory. Jesus loved to spend time alone with the Father in the natural settings that He made (Mark 1:35, Luke 22:39, John 8:1).

Questions:

1) Why does God say that we are without excuse after seeing nature?
2) When can you spend some time alone with God in His creation?
3) Which part of creation most inspires you to be in awe of God?
4) Who can you share some of these verses with this week?

Deeper Study:

Psalm 19. The sky proclaims the glory of God day after day.
Job 39:1-30. God describes His sustaining power in nature.

Genesis 1:1-2:3. This world was designed by God, and it displays His unparalleled creativity.

Exodus 14:10-22. God's power over natural forces exemplifies His sovereignty.

Prayer:

All powerful God, You reign over the earth. Thank You for the gift of Your creation. I'm fed, comforted, amazed, and humbled by the work of Your hand. I see Your power and acknowledge Your presence as I worship You. You are worthy of my devotion and honor. Help me to find You as I lift up my eyes to You today. In Jesus' name I pray. Amen.

4)   THE LORD OF THE UNIVERSE

Passage: Psalm 147:3-5

He heals the brokenhearted and binds up their wounds. He determines the number of the stars and calls them each by name. Great is our Lord and mighty in power; his understanding has no limit.

Insight:

My wife and I traveled to the ocean because we both knew we needed to mourn. When you have several miscarriages, despair wants to be your closest friend and distracts you from God's goodness in the midst of sorrow. We needed a change of scenery to process the tremendous ache of disappointment. Life can be headed one way with profound excitement, and then another direction when you realize a door is closed and dreams are crushed. The thrilling anticipation we felt from a positive pregnancy test and then the grief we felt months later when the doctor looked us in the eyes to tell us that the baby had no pulse threw us into an emotional crevasse. It is at those times that we find solace not in our feelings of misery, but in the One who receives our tears and gives us a greater perspective and perseverance. The ocean and the sky pointed us to God who is compassionate and yet eternal.

The Psalmist writes that no one has power and strength like our God. He is able to gather the exiles, heal the brokenhearted, determine the name and location of the stars, and has no limit to His understanding. Look to God as you appreciate what He has made in creation. In your walk with Him, don't lose the deep wonder that is fitting for such an incredible God. The transcendent God above us is also the immanent God who embraces us in our pain. Jesus is a man of many sorrows and is well acquainted with grief (Isaiah 53:3).

Stars are not scattered throughout the universe randomly. God cares for the stars, and He knows them each by name. They are arranged in galaxies. The earth is part of the Milky

Way galaxy. Stars are just one part of the vast work of God's hand in creation. There are billions of stars in our galaxy-the sun is just one of those stars. We share the same purpose as each of these stars: to bring God glory. Even though the sun moves at an estimated 150 miles per second,[2] it would still take the sun hundreds of millions of years to travel across the entire galaxy. That is one big galaxy! Our minds can barely comprehend the size of our own galaxy, but scientists teach that billions of galaxies exist, and they are finding new galaxies all of the time. In a similar way, we are constantly discovering new aspects of the expansive grace of God. Only God could design and sustain such a universe, and at the same time, only God could offer this amount of grace!

Application:

In Psalm 147, we learn that God cares for the earth, the grass, the cattle, and the ravens. How much more does He know and care for you (Matthew 6:25-34 and Luke 12:22-34 remind us how worrying is unnecessary and unhelpful)! God actually knows you better than you know yourself—He is the expert. Your knowledge of yourself might seem big, but it's very small compared with how well God knows you. He is both Comforter and Creator. God knows everything about you and He loves you. God knows when to call us home and how to heal the brokenhearted. You can trust Him with your needs.

Questions:

1) How does looking at the sky, made by the Lord of the universe, give you confidence in God?
2) What helps you to not worry or be swallowed by discouragement?
3) Is there anything blocking you from accessing God's strength and wisdom in your life?
4) In what ways have you experienced God's comfort?

Deeper Study:

Isaiah 40:1-31. The incomparable God brings comfort to His people.

Romans 11:33-36. God's knowledge and understanding leaves us in awe.

Job 38:1-18. God's superior wisdom puts us in our rightful place.

Isaiah 55:6-13. God's Word never returns to Him without fulfilling His plan.

Psalm 145. Notice God's character and His faithfulness to every generation.

Prayer:

Father God, You amaze me. My brain can barely grasp what You have put together in this universe. Your hands are good and strong. I pray that I would trust You more in my decisions and my actions. I want to worship You with wonder and awe. I bow down before You. You are my Maker. You know me in every aspect. I thank You today for your great love. I pray this in Jesus' name. Amen.

5)   CONQUERING YOUR OBSTACLES

Passage: Haggai 1:7

> *This is what the Lord Almighty says: "Give careful thought to your ways."*

Insight:

Do you ever get overwhelmed by a challenge in life that feels too big to overcome? The Israelites were returning from exile in Babylon. They started rebuilding the temple for God because it had been destroyed by the Babylonians. They began their work but then hit the pause button for 16 years. Instead of serving God, they focused on themselves, building their own homes while neglecting God's house. They were stuck in a spiritual dead-end and needed help to get beyond some of their hurdles. Can you relate to their struggle?

Johann Sebastian Bach was a composer who relied on God. His music was an expression of his faith, and He knew that God gave creativity and inspiration. Artists, like everyone else, can face major obstacles in their labor. Many accounts describe how he literally wrote INJ (*In Nomine Jesu*-In the name of Jesus) and SDG (*Soli Deo Gloria*- For the glory of God) on his compositions.[3] In the majority of his works, he sought God; may we have the same motives in our endeavors. Bach met with God in prayer and wrote beautiful music with a purpose to glorify God. In the same way, we can bring our work, our talents, and our ideas before God and receive His guidance. Hope comes when we remember that God is greater than any challenge we face, and His grace gives us a supply of hope far beyond our own resources.

Application:

We all have obstacles that prevent us from growing spiritually. With only our own strength, we are limited. We can get discouraged and also continue to deny our potential, but God has better plans for us. He desires healing, longing to show compassion, and His restoration makes all things new. God wants to give us a vision of what life can look like beyond our hurdles. He lovingly and firmly guided the Israelites past their obstacles and restored the people. It's when we give God full access to our lives that we begin to see that His power removes barriers. Here are three major hurdles that God can lead you through with His strength:

1) **Your Past:** If we focus on our past failures, we can beat ourselves up unnecessarily in ways that God never wants. The results can be miserable. God wants us to receive His forgiveness through Jesus and move forward with His grace. We can have a healthy contrition without being bound by guilt. On the other hand, if our past was outstanding, we need to be careful not to envy it. We can miss our current opportunities and blessings because we are fixated on past successes.

2) **Your Procrastination:** Have you ever noticed how easy it is to procrastinate? I remember as a student not getting my assignments completed on time or frequently waiting until literally the last minute instead of doing it during an earlier, calmer time. It's been said that "hard work" is simply "easy work" not done at the right time. The Israelites knew what they were supposed to do in building the temple, but they kept putting it off until 16 years had passed. Procrastination became a pattern in my life, and it wasn't easy to break it. The Holy Spirit can teach us new ways.

3) **Your Priorities:** Our priorities won't stay hidden. They will emerge in our prayers, how we handle our money, how we spend our time and energy, and in our relationships. In this passage, the Israelites fell into a 'me-first' attitude. They wanted to take care of their own

houses first, and eventually they might later think about God or other people in the community. They were apathetic spiritually because deep down they were acting selfishly. God was helping them to overcome this obstacle, and they made a great adjustment with their internal motivations and priorities.

Questions:

1) Why is procrastinating so easy to do? What helps you conquer it?
2) Are there any priorities in your life that need to be changed?
3) When has God given you a positive vision of your potential?
4) How does Jesus help you to be less selfish?

Deeper Study:

Read the book of Haggai- it's one of the shortest books in the Bible. You are not less spiritual if you need the table of contents to find it! Write down examples of the three hurdles mentioned earlier in this chapter. Also, write down how they were able to overcome these common obstacles with God's help.

Haggai 1:2-8. Listen for God's timing and avoid selfish motives.

Haggai 1:13-14. When God stirs you to take action, don't delay.

Haggai 2:3-4. Don't let the success of other people intimidate you.

Haggai 2:7-9. God has all of the resources and peace that you need.

Prayer:

Gracious God, thank You for helping me to see the obstacles that are blocking me spiritually. I want to overcome them with Your help. I believe in Your wisdom and Your power. May Your Holy Spirit fill me now, stir me up, and make me whole. I pray this in Your name Jesus. Amen.

6)   THE BOLDNESS OF JESUS

Passage: John 8:58

> *"I tell you the truth," Jesus answered, "before Abraham was born, I am!"*

Insight:

As an example, I remember going cliff diving with a group of friends in college. There were a wide range of options regarding the height of the jumps, and testosterone was definitely a factor in choosing launch points. I would like to think it was more from wisdom than fear that I decided to dive from reasonable heights. If someone backed down from a diving point on the canyon, his return to a lower height was called "the walk of shame" (you can probably detect that this story is a description of my experience, not a recommendation). Some friends who were experienced divers would stand at the top of the cliff and prepare to dive. There was a buzz in the air because of their boldness. When Jesus spoke, I think there was a similar buzz as people contemplated the meaning of His words and actions.

Early in my spiritual exploration, even though I studied the life of Jesus and was impressed, I still didn't want to follow Him. I knew it was a major decision, and I didn't want to make the commitment. I wanted to make sure that I felt like I could really trust Jesus. It's possible to know He is good, yet at the same time resist Him. How is admiring Jesus from a distance different than walking closely with Him? No person could simply persuade me to follow Jesus, but the decision came after spending time reflecting on His life, teaching, and love. God changed my heart, and I realized that nothing in my life could compare to Him and what He was offering.

God is the source of all grace. Understanding grace begins with appreciating God. In the book of Exodus, chapter 3 verse 14, God introduces Himself to Moses with the personal name, "I AM WHO I AM". The Israelites know that the name "I AM" is God's name, but a pious Jew, in reverence, would not even write out the full name. So when Jesus makes the statement that He existed before Abraham, He is telling the crowd that He is God. It would have been tempting to deny this fact to please the crowd, but the grace of Jesus is grounded in truth. Jesus was not created—He always existed! Grace doesn't water down the substance of the message of Jesus. There are seven additional times in the gospel of John that Jesus makes an "I AM" statement. Why does Jesus want everyone to know that He is fully human and fully God? Notice the everyday images Jesus uses in His descriptions of Himself as He invites us to get to know Him personally.

Application:

Here are the seven "I AM" statements from Jesus in John's gospel:

1) "I am the bread of life. He who comes to me will never go hungry, and he who believes in me will never be thirsty." Read John 6:35.

2) "I am the light of the world. Whoever follows me will never walk in darkness, but will have the light of life." Read John 8:12.

3) "I am the gate; whoever enters through me will be saved. He will come in and go out and find pasture." Read John 10:9.

4) "I am the good shepherd. The good shepherd lays down his life for the sheep." Read John 10:11.

5) "I am the resurrection and the life. He who believes in me will live, even though he dies; and whoever lives and believes in me will never die. Do you believe this?" Read John 11:25-26.

6) "I am the way and the truth and the life. No one comes to the Father except through me." Read John 14:6.

7) "I am the vine; you are the branches. If a man remains in me and I in him, he will bear much fruit; apart from me you can do nothing." Read John 15:5.

Questions:

1) Which statement of Jesus do you think is the most difficult for people to accept today?
2) What do you learn about Jesus from each statement?
3) Which 'I am' statement is the most encouraging to hear in your life situation now?
4) What insights do you gain about Jesus from the imagery he uses?

Deeper Study:

John 1:1-14. Jesus is God; and through Him all things were made.

Hebrews 13:8. Jesus is reliable in an unreliable world.

1 Peter 2:1-12. Jesus is good and wants to be the cornerstone of our lives.

Luke 4:14-21. Jesus is spreading good news and proclaiming freedom.

Acts 9:1-31. Christianity is about a very personal relationship with Jesus.

Prayer:

God, thank You for Your Son Jesus who gives constant grace and strength. Taking my focus off of myself and putting it on You is what I'm designed to do. I pray that my faith in You will grow, Jesus, as I dwell on the truth about how good You really are. I want to bring You as much glory as possible. I have made the decision that You are my Savior, and I want to follow You. I pray this in Your name Lord. Amen.

CULTIVATING GRACE

God alone satisfies our spiritual thirst

7)   BIBLE STUDY WITH A PURPOSE

Passage: Acts 8:30-31

Then Philip ran up to the chariot and heard the man reading Isaiah the prophet. "Do you understand what you are reading?" Philip asked. "How can I," he said, "unless someone explains it to me?" So he invited Philip to come up and sit with him.

Insight:

There have been certain classes in school for me that were intimidating: Latin in junior high school, calculus in high school, and Greek in graduate school are near the top of the list. There were other topics that I avoided: I didn't take any math in college because I didn't have to. Many people view the Bible as ancient, confusing, and best to avoid. I never opened the Bible during the first eighteen years of my life, so I can relate to having no desire to read it. As I look back now, I'm so grateful that those misleading feelings didn't keep me from discovering God's Word. It is a treasure; but in today's culture, it's easy to ignore such a wonderful and untapped gift. God's grace flows out of Scripture, and reading the Bible is one habit that allows us to consistently draw from God's refreshing fountain.

God communicates to us personally in this love letter that is the Bible. Have you ever had a strong desire to know God better? The Ethiopian man wanted to learn more about God, so he began reading the Bible. But there was one problem: he didn't understand what he was reading. Have you ever opened up the Bible, started reading, and couldn't make any sense of it at all? Don't feel bad. Even the apostle Peter mentions that some of Paul's writings can be difficult to understand (2 Peter 3:15-16). But, even though it can be difficult, it is still worth the effort. Some of the best things in life come with perseverance, and the Holy Spirit will enlighten you as you read.

Application:

As a child, my grandparents challenged me each day I was with them to write down something I saw, something I learned, and one way in which I helped someone. It gave me a new perspective on my day. In a similar way, practical tools make it easier to understand God's Word and discover His grace:

1) **Pray** before you read and ask the Holy Spirit to help give you insight into the Scripture. God will shed light on His Word. 1 Corinthians 2:6-16, John 14:24-26, and 1 John 2:27 are some of the verses that explain how the Holy Spirit gives you spiritual understanding.

2) **Find a friend** who can help you as you read. Philip was able to come alongside the Ethiopian and teach him about the book of Isaiah. Look for a friend who is strong in their faith and can read with you and discuss the passage. In college, Mike Helton met with me every morning, and we read through the gospel of Matthew together, a few verses at a time. Brian Birdsall also faithfully walked me through the Bible. I know I asked these men hundreds of questions, but they were very patient with me.

3) **Get connected to a healthy church** that teaches from the Word of God. Choose a church where you are spiritually fed.

4) **Check out some resources** like the *NIV Study Bible, NIV Life Application Bible,* or commentaries that explain passages in greater depth. You can purchase these at a Christian bookstore or by ordering them on the Internet. You can also find free eBibles and Bible Apps which are great options.

5) **Make it a priority** to add time for God's Word in your daily schedule. Your faith grows as you spend time reading the Bible; you can't live on bread alone; the Word is our spiritual food. Get some good meals. Dive into Scripture and God will meet you there. Then apply His truth to your life.

Questions:

Consider these helpful questions as you read the Bible:

1) What does the passage teach you about God?
2) Are there any examples to follow or anything to avoid?
3) What statements are encouraging in the passage? Are there any promises?
4) Noticing key words, what is the basic message of the passage?
5) Are there any verses you want to memorize or use for meditation?
6) What difference does this make in your life? How can you apply it now?
7) What do the verses teach you about people and relationships?
8) What parts of the passage are not clear?
9) Are there any other verses that are similar to this passage?
10) Who can you share this passage with during the week?

Deeper Study:

2 Timothy 3:16-17. The Bible is God's Word and is completely reliable.

Psalm 1:1-3. Meditating on Scripture will bear fruit in your life.

Romans 10:16-17. Your faith can grow by listening to God's Word.

Psalm 119:103-105. You will gain understanding and guidance for your decisions.

1 Peter 1:23-25. The Word of God is eternal; it stands forever.

Hebrews 4:12. The Bible can penetrate your innermost being.

Prayer:

God, thank You for the Bible and the insight You give me as I read it. Help me to apply what I learn so I can live it during the week. I pray this in Jesus' name. Amen.

8)   AN APPETITE FOR GOD

Passage: Psalm 42:1-2

As the deer pants for streams of water, so my soul pants for you, O God. My soul thirsts for God, for the living God. When can I go and meet with God?

Insight:

There is no substitute for experiencing the presence of God. If I'm only serving God and not drawing near to Him, I can get very dry and shallow in my relationship with God. Does that ever happen to you? Busyness without connection to God is one common way that burnout happens. There have always been people in my life that have helped me get back on track in this area; the temptation for me to become too focused on serving is very real every week. I remember starting out in ministry with so much zeal, and my mentor, Carl expressing, "The work you do for God will never go deeper than your relationship with Him." Those words still echo inside of me often!

Picture a deer exceeding 400 pounds and having a large number of antlers; this is no Bambi level of thirst! The psalmist who wrote the above passage had no weak or small hunger for God. He was a "son of Korah" which was the Levitical choir appointed by David to serve in the temple. Today's equivalent would be a worship leader. This is a very honest and vulnerable psalm written by someone in a leadership position. Long-term followers of Jesus and leaders have struggles in their faith and their walks with God. The author of Psalm 42 didn't hide what was happening in his life; he put it out there for us to read. The Bible doesn't cover up the human side of our faith: it gives us raw honesty. You will notice the author is depressed since five times he used the words downcast, despair, or disturbed. The psalmist was often in tears as he was surrounded by people taunting him, yet he continued to praise God and expressed his thirst for God in the deepest way. It's truly an inspiring example of someone who has learned how to cherish God and the grace of His presence.

Application:

1) **Self-sufficiency is too heavy a burden to carry.** The psalmist admitted to God that he needed heavenly help. When we don't try to manage everything on our own, pressure begins to roll off our shoulders onto the One who can carry the stress for us.

2) **Have spiritual longings that won't be satisfied too easily.** We often find food, television, sleep, or drugs to replace an experience with God. Have more than just a token desire to know God.

3) **Hope from God is more real than your feelings.** Like us, the psalmist's feelings wavered between praise and lament. God's hope is present the entire time, but it is often closer and more reliable than it feels. Don't let our feelings lead us; that is Jesus' role.

4) **The wrong "carrot" leads to the wrong destination.** Everyone is chasing some kind of "carrot" in life. The psalmist rid himself of misleading goals, so God is his main pursuit. If we chase the wrong prize in life, we will usually end up in the wrong place.

5) **Savor your time in God's presence.** God is refreshment for the weary, love for the lonely, a rock for the insecure, peace for the soul, a song for the downcast, and help for the one who is outnumbered.

Questions:

1) When have you been thirsty for God?
2) When can you trust your feelings?
3) What are some of the things that you are chasing now?
4) What have been your richest times in God's presence?

Deeper Study:

Psalm 84. Take time to draw near to God during your day.

Jeremiah 2:13. There is no adequate substitute for having God in your life.

John 4:1-26. Empty religion pales in comparison with knowing Jesus.

Exodus 33:12-18. Seek God's face more than His hand.

Song Of Songs 2:4. Realize how much God loves you and receive His love.

Prayer:

Heavenly Father, I confess that I often try to find substitutes in my life instead of seeking You. Forgive me for trying to look more spiritual around people than I really am. From the deepest parts of my being, I cry out to You now. I have no real hope without You. Draw near to me, Lord, as I draw near to You. I praise You in Jesus name. Amen.

9)   LISTENING TO GOD

Passage: 1 Samuel 3:8-10

> *The Lord called Samuel a third time, and Samuel got up and went to Eli and said, "Here I am; you called me." Then Eli realized that the Lord was calling the boy. So Eli told Samuel, "Go and lie down, and if he calls you, say, 'Speak, Lord, for your servant is listening.'" So Samuel went and lay down in his place. The Lord came and stood there, calling as at the other times, "Samuel! Samuel!" Then Samuel said, "Speak, for your servant is listening."*

Insight:

The year was 2005, and we had just moved to Southern California. The house prices in San Diego were shocking to us. Many people had said that we needed to bite the bullet and just buy a house. We found a house that we were both excited to purchase. In my mind, it was a done deal. My wise wife suggested, "Let's keep praying about this." We had no idea that the housing market was about to crash. I kept thinking about the size of the house, the location, and the great views. Because I had gone to the prospective house so many times, I had become attached to the house and it didn't feel good to step away from purchasing it. Sometimes God's grace includes protecting us from enticing decisions that are destructive. Our inner turmoil would soon be resolved. There was no audible voice, but a deep sense that we didn't have a green light from God. I admit that I don't always listen closely enough to God. We eventually withdrew our potential offer though because it didn't feel like God wanted us to close the deal. I look back now after many years of renting and know that God helped us to avoid a purchase we couldn't afford to make. The promptings of the Holy Spirit are an example of how God personally leads us as His children.

Accessing God's grace and voice may include slowing down and giving Him our full attention without distractions. God spoke to Samuel, but Samuel did not know how to listen to God yet. Eli began to teach Samuel how to listen to God. It is one of the most important skills in our spiritual lives. If we don't listen to God, then we can make the wrong decisions and run ahead of God's timing. Saul is someone who failed to inquire of God (1 Chronicles 13:3), and his life took a downward spiral. In a time of battle, however, David was careful to check in with God and ask not only what decision to make but also how to carry out the plan. (1 Chronicles 14:8-17). The Bible has three 'God is' statements: "God is love (1 John 4:16), God is light (1 John 1:5), and God is a consuming fire (Hebrews 12:28-29)." These positive attributes of our Creator are worth taking time to reflect on today. In what ways do these three attributes point us to His grace? How do these descriptions of God encourage us to listen closely to Him?

Application:

As a reflection of His grace, God communicates with you in so many different ways. God personally guides you with His Word, His Spirit, and His voice. The primary revelation you have is through the Bible. God also speaks through His Spirit: teaching, rebuking, and giving insight and direction. Another way God talks is through His people. Surround yourself with wise people who can speak truth into your life. God can also use circumstances creatively, as well as nature, dreams, and even angels to bring you His message. As you spend time reading the Bible and praying, one option is to grab a pen and paper to write down what God is communicating to you.

Eli's advice for listening to God:

1) **Be Still.** Eli told Samuel, "Go and lie down": Psalm 46:10 also tells you to be still and know that He is God. So be still. Turn off interruptions like your cell phone and

your computer and your TV and begin to tune into God. Find a place where you can humble yourself before God.

2) **Be Patient.** Eli added the phrase: "...And if He calls you". Don't try to force it or pretend like God is communicating if He is not telling you anything. You don't have to try to be extra spiritual. Job said that there are times when we don't hear His direction (Job 23:8-10). Don't be discouraged. God knows when He wants to speak.

3) **Be Open.** Eli explained, "Say, 'Speak, for your servant is listening'. " Don't just say this phrase, mean it. This phrase tells God that you desire His direction, and it also communicates that you are humble before Him. You truly want to do whatever He says. You are listening as a servant. When you hear His voice, act on it because He is leading you with grace and wisdom.

Questions:

1) Do you spend more time talking to God or listening?
2) Do you have a favorite place where you can be quiet and just listen?
3) What is your attitude when you hear God's Word- are you teachable?
4) What are the biggest distractions that are hindering you spiritually?
5) What has God been communicating to you recently?

Deeper Study:

John 16:14-16. The Holy Spirit communicates and teaches you about Jesus.

Proverbs 12:15. If you don't listen to God, you will make foolish decisions.

Hebrews 4:12-13. The Word of God penetrates the heart and gives life.

John 17:14-17. The Bible is God's truth—it has the power to change your life.

Luke 10:38-42. Serving God shouldn't replace listening closely to Him.

Prayer:

Loving God, thank You for wanting to hear me and also help me listen to You. Thank You for Your many ways of communicating with me and getting my attention. You are worthy of my undistracted time and attention. Please help me to be someone who hears You and then does what You say. I want to know You better and be sensitive to the promptings of Your Holy Spirit. I pray this in Your name Jesus. Amen.

10) CONNECTING WITH A CHURCH FAMILY

Passage: Hebrews 10:25

> *Let us not give up meeting together, as some are in the habit of doing, but let us encourage one another-and all the more as you see the Day approaching.*

Insight:

I went to graduate school in Dallas, Texas, and knew that I needed a church home during my years there. There were so many good churches close to our school. I spent a few months exploring different congregations until I found Concord Church. The preaching was inspiring, the people were so welcoming, and the worship was passionate. Coming from a smaller Presbyterian church to a large congregation of several thousand people was a big change for me. I remember my first Sunday there—I was the only person who wasn't African-American, but I just knew I was in the right place. I learned so much at Concord that I would never have studied at seminary. I'm so grateful for how God blesses us and enriches our faith through a wide range of churches that demonstrate His love and goodness! God has designed the church to be an instrument to extend His grace in our lives.

Unfortunately, many people have had negative experiences in church and understandably have not returned because the wounds run so deep. Healing can be a process and involve some courageous steps. Be discerning as you go to a new church. God knows that we usually struggle in our faith when we are not connected with other people who truly love God. As much as we try to build our faith alone, the fact is that we need each other. One tangible example of this is the decision we make each week regarding church. Spiritual decisions include simply choosing to be in places that bolster and cultivate our faith. God doesn't want us to miss the blessings that are a part of a healthy church family. A church is about the people and the relationships much more than the building. One major indicator that we are in a healthy church is that we are growing there in the grace of God.

Application:

What are some key qualities to look for in a church?

1) **A church that is through the roof (Mark 2:1-12).** Notice how the four friends cared for the paralytic, they even broke through a roof for him. A church is designed to be a place of healing and brings people to Jesus. The friends are very loving and determined in this passage. A church can physically take care of people and also carry them to Jesus through prayer. In our church recently, people persevered in prayer for a boy who had necrotizing fasciitis (a flesh-eating disease), and God miraculously healed him.

2) **A church that is not in a cave (1 Kings 19:3-9).** Elijah was scared, discouraged, and hiding from the world. The bottom line was that he was wrapped up in himself too much and had stared too long at his problems. A church needs to be courageous in reaching out, not selfish or intimidated by the world.

3) **A church that is in many jars (Joel 2:28-29 and 2 Corinthians 4:7).** God celebrates diversity, and we should too. Look at the passage in Joel and the range of people who have received the Holy Spirit to minister. Even though we have bodies, like a clay jar, with physical challenges, God has placed His treasured Holy Spirit in us.

4) **A church that is not collecting dust (2 Kings 22:8-2 Kings 23:3).** In this passage, the Israelites were in a spiritual funk as they had wandered away from the Scriptures. Sadly, God's Word was collecting dust in the temple. Fortunately, their king named Josiah insisted that the nation turn to God and return to the Word. Their faith became alive again as they were

inspired by the Scriptures. A church is responsible to accurately teach from the Bible and give people good spiritual food to eat.

As you look for a church:

1) Remember that every church has issues and struggles; be gracious.
2) Look for a church that actually teaches the Bible during their services.
3) Make sure their doctrine is consistent with the Bible.
4) Stay away from hypocrisy and churches that are self-righteous.
5) Get connected in Bible studies and discover a way to serve when you find a good church.
6) Find a church where the people are loving, and you also sense God's Holy Spirit there.

Questions:

1) Have you had good or bad experiences at church?
2) Do you have a church home now where you are really connected?
3) Why do you think so many people skip church?
4) Why do you think God doesn't want us to miss church?
5) How has participating in a church changed your life?
6) Is there anyone you can invite to church this week?

Deeper Study:

Acts 2:42-47. This passage covers the DNA of a healthy church.

Acts 20:27-38. There should be deep bonds within a church family.

1 Corinthians 13:1-13. A church's purpose includes demonstrating Jesus' love.

1 Timothy 3:1-16. There are character qualifications for church leadership.

2 John 1:4-6. Make sure you continue to walk in truth, obedience, and love.

Prayer:

Father God, thank You for the churches in my city. I pray today that You would bless the pastors and leaders in all of the churches. I pray for the wisdom to know which church should be my church family. Please help me to get connected. I don't want to skip church; I want to stay faithful to You and grow in my faith. Help me to have the right attitude at church so I don't miss out on time with You or blessings from You. I pray this in Your name Jesus. Amen.

11) AN EXPRESSION OF NEW LIFE

Passage: Matthew 28:18-20

> *Then Jesus came to them and said, "All authority in heaven and on earth has been given to me. Therefore go and make disciples of all nations, baptizing them in the name of the Father and of the Son and of the Holy Spirit, and teaching them to obey everything I have commanded you. And surely I am with you always, to the very end of the age."*

Insight:

For several years after becoming a Christian I was perplexed about baptism because I had heard some very negative teaching on the topic. A small group of people that I later learned was a cult pressured me, claiming that they were the only "true Christians" in the world. Needless to say, their views of baptism were not Biblically based and produced a significant amount of confusion. It took time and searching the Scripture before my mindset was transformed, the damage healed, and I was thinking clearly again. A maligned and very difficult topic for me became a strong desire to move forward in my faith. When I did get baptized, it was a real celebration! I invited many of my friends and shared my journey before the baptism. Since then, I have had the privilege of baptizing many people, and every one of them has had such a pure joy (even when the water temperature was much colder than anticipated!).

There are a few rituals that Jesus emphasizes in the Bible, one of them is water baptism. It's both a command to His followers and a time of great celebration. Interestingly, grace can be given through a command. How often do we forget that the commands of God bring joy? Jesus makes it clear that He wants all of His followers to be baptized in water. We can't earn our way to heaven through water baptism. We are welcomed into heaven because Jesus died for our sins and is risen, not because of anything we do. Water baptism honors Jesus and is a time of identification and closeness with our Savior. Baptism and communion incorporate our physical participation in His grace.

Application:

Here are some practical tips in getting past some common excuses:

1) Some people think water baptism is just a suggestion, but in fact it's a command by Jesus. It's how we publicly identify with Him.

2) Some people think that they don't need to be baptized right away, but in the Scripture, there is an urgency to do it right away (Acts chapter 16). Don't let unnecessary delays get in the way between you and God.

3) Some people are timid when it comes to baptism. Jesus said to acknowledge Him before people and he will acknowledge you before the Father (Matthew 10:32). That's enough motivation to overcome any fear. Don't be ashamed of Jesus. Also, thinking that you must be perfect in order to be baptized is a misconception (or none of us would be baptized this side of heaven). Let His grace guide you as you consider baptism.

4) Some people will be persecuted if baptized. This is unfortunate, but baptism and obedience are worth any cost.

5) Some people dread getting immersed in water. It might be out of our comfort zone, but I have never seen anyone be baptized without tremendous joy afterwards.

Questions:

1) Have you put your trust in Jesus to be your Savior?
2) Have you been water baptized?
3) What are some of the reasons in the Bible to be baptized?

4)   Is there anyone you can encourage to be baptized?

5)   How much joy has there been in the baptisms you have seen?

Deeper Study:

Matthew 3:13-17. Jesus was baptized and set the example for us.

Romans 6:1-14. Baptism reflects unity with Jesus and receiving a fresh start.

Acts 16:13-15. We affirm our faith in Jesus through water baptism.

Acts 16:31-34. Water baptism happens right after conversion with great joy.

Prayer:

Father God, thank You for the ritual of water baptism. Thank You that Jesus was baptized to set the example. I know you want me to be baptized, and I want to respond by saying "yes." I also would like to encourage other Christians to be baptized too. Thank You that there is so much joy in being baptized. I love You Jesus and this is all for You. I pray this in Your name, Lord. Amen.

12) FOLLOWING JESUS TODAY

Passage: Luke 5:8-11

*When Simon Peter saw this, he fell at Jesus' knees
and said, "Go away from me, Lord; I am a sinful man!"
For he and all his companions were astonished at the
catch of fish they had taken, and so were James and
John, the sons of Zebedee, Simon's partners. Then
Jesus said to Simon, "Don't be afraid; from now on
you will catch men." So they pulled their boats up on
shore, left everything and followed him.*

Insight:

I'm privileged to work with compassionate people who serve
free meals in our community. I've also seen other people travel
overseas to serve in a hospital, provide a shower ministry to
homeless people, visit elderly people in a local convalescent
home, care for children, and encourage prisoners in jail. There
is a very positive golden thread in these acts of service: they
are motivated by grace! Maybe you can relate to an inner drive
that is derived out of love? Sadly, history is full of people who
have used religion and Jesus' name to justify vile behavior. In
contrast, when you let God's grace fill your heart, you are
capable of the most God-glorifying actions. Jesus will lead you
to places and people that are ready to receive your timely help.

Experiencing God's grace usually involves making some
intentional decisions. Peter was a professional fisherman who
had been trying to catch fish all night but caught nothing. When
Jesus showed up and told Peter where to drop the nets, he
didn't want to listen to Jesus. His pride didn't want any
instructions from Jesus (ever notice how pride hates
suggestions and can insist on sticking to a plan that doesn't
work?). When he simply did what Jesus told him to do, the
catch of fish was so abundant that Peter was humbled. Jesus
told Peter that greater work is coming. Soon Peter will be
reaching men and women for God. Following Jesus is more

than just a noble concept; it includes real choices in our everyday lives.

Application:

There are major lessons in this passage about following Jesus:

1) **Following Jesus includes realizing that He has more wisdom than you in every area of life.** We are often tempted to think that we are the experts and have a better plan than God; we try to call the shots.

2) **Following Jesus includes a sense of urgency.** We are often tempted to think that we will wholeheartedly follow Jesus down the road when it's convenient and easier. Jesus says that life with Him is more abundant than any cheap thrills the world can offer.

3) **Following Jesus includes being willing to leave everything.** We are often tempted to put certain people or things in our life above what God wants us to do. Jesus is worthy of being the center of our lives.

4) **Following Jesus includes leading people to Him.** We are often tempted to think it's only about ourselves and ignore other people and their souls. Everyone makes their own decisions and many people reject God, but God still wants each person to know how much He loves them.

5) **Following Jesus includes believing He will do great things through you.** We are often tempted to think that we are failures, but God speaks kindly to us and doesn't give up on us. God rewards anyone who earnestly seeks Him.

Questions:

1) What are some of the reasons to follow Jesus?
2) Do you ever say no to Jesus or think you have a better plan?
3) Has God ever humbled you with unexpected results?

4)   What is Jesus asking you to do or say this week?

Deeper Study:

Luke 8:22-25. Jesus can calm you and your storms.

Matthew 16:24-27. Some people gain the whole world but forfeit their soul.

John 21:15-25. Focus on following Jesus, not your past failures.

Hebrews 11:1-40. Be encouraged by these examples of faith.

Joshua 1:6-9. Be courageous when God is leading you.

Prayer:

Father God, thank You for sending Your Son Jesus to earth. I am challenged to really follow You Jesus, and not let my pride get in the way. I know what You are asking me to do, and I want to stop resisting. So today I commit myself to You, and I want to do and say exactly what You want. You are the Lord of my entire life. I pray this in Your name, Jesus. Amen.

HEALING GRACE

God repairs our brokenness

13) GOD'S REACH CAN TOUCH YOUR LOWEST POINTS

Passage: Numbers 11:23

> *The Lord answered Moses, "Is the Lord's arm too short? You will now see whether or not what I say will come true for you."*

Insight:

One of the lowest points of my life occurred when I nearly died from toxic levels of a prescribed medication. I was playing professional soccer in Zimbabwe at the time. My physician gave me the well-known medication to prevent the possibility of contracting malaria. Unfortunately, I had an extreme adverse reaction to the drug. My body was unable to process the medication, resulting in toxic levels of the drug inside of my body. Some of my symptoms included vision problems, massive fatigue, migraine headaches, mood swings, bizarre dreams, and several cardiac abnormalities. My heart would sometimes beat 160 times a minute while I was resting, including an atrial flutter. The results included many serious and complex health issues, and there were no answers regarding a possible recovery. It was like a constant storm; I felt like a table that had its legs removed quickly and shattered on the ground. The experience was an absolute nightmare (literally at times), and made me wonder, "What do I still have left?"

My soccer career was finished, and my recovery process took many years. In chapters 6 and 23 in the book of Job, he cries out that his anguish and misery couldn't be weighed on the scale. The levels of pain in his life were indescribable and off the charts. My challenges were smaller than what Job went through, but those verses really resonated with me. There were times in my struggle when I didn't feel that God was there. By His grace though, God can bring good things out of the cruelest trials. Ironically, my illness became the time in my life when my faith eventually grew the most, and God also used my illness to redirect me into ministry. At that point, I fully realized that if I was able to live or if something good came out of my life, it would be by the grace of God.

There is absolutely no situation or part of your life that can't be reached by the grace of God! Nothing is too difficult for God. Moses was leading an estimated 2 million people in the desert when God said He would provide food including meat for the next month. Moses, one of the greatest spiritual leaders, didn't believe this was possible. Moses knew that no person was able to feed everyone, but Moses initially underestimated what God could do. God asked Moses the question in this verse, implying that certainly God's arm was not too short to accomplish this goal. Sometimes we forget how God can reach down and what He can bring into our lives. God still cares for you when no one else is able to help you. God will not abandon you in the darkest or most terrifying hour.

Application:

Look at some of the ways that God reaches down to us in difficult situations. Take some time to read and consider the following passages:

1) **Loneliness And Fear:** Read Genesis chapter 16 and observe how God sees Hagar, a single mom, and provides for her when she runs out of hope and supplies.

2) **Rejection:** Read Jeremiah chapter 38 and notice how the prophet Jeremiah was innocent but thrown into a deep well and left there to starve to death. God provides a man named Ebed-Melech who notices Jeremiah and gathers a group of people to lift him to safety.

3) **Dishonesty:** Read Luke chapter 19 and discover how Zacchaeus lied to people and took advantage of people, yet Jesus still wanted to spend time with him.

4) **Despair:** Read Psalm 40 and hear how David sunk into depression, but God lifted him out of the muddy pit and gave him a firm place to stand.

5) **Impurity:** Read John chapter 8 and study how Jesus finds a woman who was caught in adultery. Jesus responds graciously to her and tells her also to go and sin no more. She receives a fresh start to her life.

6) **Pain And Demons:** Read Mark chapter 5 and picture how Jesus heals a demon-possessed man and rescues him from the thrashing he has endured.

7) **Death And Grieving:** Read John chapter 11 and see how Jesus speaks into the tomb of Lazarus and with His voice calls Lazarus out of the grave. Jesus then comforts the mourners with His presence and promises.

Questions:

1) Which of the seven examples listed above is similar to your situation?

2) Why is God so willing to enter into the most painful and confusing moments of your life?

3) When has God surprised you with His power?

4) Do you know anyone who would benefit from your encouragement this week?

Deeper Study:

Ephesians 3:14-21. Good roots lead to good fruit.

Matthew 14:13-21. Jesus can thoroughly satisfy those who are hungry.

2 Timothy 1:6-9. God can replace your timidity with boldness.

Nahum 1:7. Your first step forward is to trust God with your heart.

Judges 3:12-15. Don't stop praying because you made a bad decision.

Psalm 121. Lift your eyes above your situation to your strong Creator.

Prayer:

Father God, please help me to remember that Your strong arm is not too short. Forgive me for my pride in not turning to You. You know the low points in my life right now, I pray that You will bring Your hope, healing, and strength to these situations. And I pray for my friends who are in deep over their heads, rescue and encourage them I pray, Lord Jesus. I pray this in Your name, Lord. Amen.

14)   FROM HUMBLE BEGINNINGS

Passage: Esther 2:17-18

Now the king was attracted to Esther more than to any of the other women, and she won his favor and approval more than any of the other virgins. So he set a royal crown on her head and made her queen instead of Vashti. And the king gave a great banquet, Esther's banquet, for all his nobles and officials. He proclaimed a holiday throughout the provinces and distributed gifts with royal liberality.

Insight:

Many times, the famous Gospel singer Donnie McClurkin has shared his story of how he experienced tragedy at an early age. As the oldest child, he was sometimes expected to watch his two-year old brother. One day, as his younger brother was in the front yard playing, Donnie went across the street to retrieve a ball. His brother followed him, but Donnie was unaware of it. A car traveling down the road hit his brother and killed him. Can you imagine trying to manage such a heartbreaking and traumatic event? Ultimately, the love Donnie experienced from God was larger than his personal pain. God brought Donnie through times of extreme anguish and sadness, and Donnie now sings about the real hope and peace that are found in Jesus Christ. Having overcome his devastating childhood, Donnie now reaches out to millions of people with the love of Jesus through his music.[4]

God delights in showering His grace on lonely and unlikely recipients! Esther wasn't the obvious selection to be the next Queen of Persia for many reasons. She grew up in a country where, sadly, Jewish people were seen as second-class citizens. Both of her parents died when she was young. She did not have much money, status, or fame. But, God's favor is more important than all of these other factors. King Xerxes had cruelly divorced his first wife, Vashti, and was searching for a new queen. We do not know all of the details regarding how Esther viewed king Xerxes at that time. We do know, however, that she became the next queen and courageously used her influence to help rescue a nation. God can raise up any person in any situation for any of His purposes. Do not dwell on your past, trust God with your future.

Application:

In the book of Esther chapter 2, there is a loving friendship between Mordecai and his cousin Esther, and these principles are displayed:

1) Don't let massive trials stop your kindness towards other people.
2) Deep pain should not stop you from receiving love from other people.
3) Be discerning because a devoted friend will show it in their actions.
4) Unless it is immoral, honoring authority is actually a good thing.

In Esther chapter 4, Esther knows that God has raised her up to be the queen for a purpose. She has the opportunity to save the lives of her people. Her life embodies what God can do through a willing person:

1) God can redeem any situation or loss.
2) God gives you strength and courage to overcome oppression.
3) God can give you hope and arrange your future plans before you realize it.

In 1 Corinthians chapter 12, it is clear that God makes one body with many diverse parts. Everyone is important. Psalm 139 also tells us that God has made every person unique. God has beautifully created every person and has special opportunities for each person to use their gifts (Ephesians 2:10). God wants us to be confident in Him and His plan.

Questions:

1) Can you identify with a "humble beginning" during your childhood years?

2) Who has helped you to overcome your most difficult challenges?

3) How do your specific trials help you encourage other people?

4) What platforms has God given you to be a positive influence?

Deeper Study:

Jeremiah 29:11-14. God has great plans for your future.

Proverbs 19:20-23. Listen to godly advice and keep a healthy fear of the Lord.

Philippians 2:1-11. God will help you develop the same attitude as Jesus.

Psalm 75. God humbles the proud and raises up servants.

Amos 7:14-15. God will train you and provide the words to say.

Ezra 3:10-11. God can use you to rebuild what has been destroyed.

Prayer:

Father God, I thank You that You elevate everyone who is humble and You are pleased when we seek You. You know my past and my current situation, and You have a good plan for my future. Please touch my life, heal me deeply, and raise me up for Your glory. I believe that what You did for Esther and Donnie; You can also do in my life. I pray this in Jesus' Name. Amen.

15) RESTORING THE INJURED

Passage: John 9:11, 35

> *"The man they call Jesus made some mud and put it on my eyes. He told me to go to Siloam and wash. So I went and washed, and then I could see."...Jesus heard that they had thrown him out, and when he found him, he said, "Do you believe in the Son of Man?"'*

Insight:

Celebrating my seventh birthday with my parents was an event that remains in my mind today because it was my last birthday that we all spent together. They divorced soon after, and I felt completely helpless and devastated. It was something I didn't want or expect, and I couldn't do anything to prevent it from happening. As a young child, it was as if the two pillars of my life were being torn apart. I do want to add that I love my parents, feel very grateful for our relationships, and remain close to each of them. I attempted to cope with mental toughness, by excelling in academics and athletics, and getting counseling. Generally, I was working to make sense of my life. While these are not bad coping mechanisms, something was still missing. I share this with you to say; the goodness and grace of God has provided the deepest and most powerful healing for me.

God has more than enough grace to bring you through any of life's unwanted events! Not only does God have enough grace to bring you through difficulty, but enough to help you place both feet on solid ground. Injuries can remind us of our need for God's grace and healing touch. Have you experienced any major injuries physically or in your relationships? Unfortunately, many people I have talked with have deep spiritual scars based on how they were treated in a church setting. In John chapter 9, there was a blind man who was healed by Jesus but was rejected by the religious leaders. The Bible says that Jesus heard that they had thrown him out, and He went and found the man. The conversation and compassionate words of Jesus brought healing to the wounded man who was struggling in his community. It's a story that reminds us that acceptance by Jesus can overcome the stinging rejection of people.

Application:

Jesus Christ left heaven, was mistreated on earth, died on a cross while being completely innocent of any charge, and willingly paid the full price for our sins. Isn't it comforting to know that we have a high priest who can relate to our injuries? He is well acquainted with sorrows. As Savior, He is also risen from the grave, is in heaven now, and will return to reign forever as He has promised. Jesus can walk beside us and help us with the details of the issues we face in our lives. He is also able to give us scope and perspective to rise above the level of our problems, give real hope, and offer us new beginnings. The big picture is not daunting to the Lord; in fact He states confidently that He has overcome the sins of the world (John 16:33). Restoration has been demonstrated in His life, and He is an able restorer today in our challenges!

Historically speaking, the church was the most vibrant and experienced the deepest levels of unity when there was an increase in persecution. What are the reasons for that surprising truth? The outward circumstances of our lives don't have the final say: because of God's grace, great blessings can emerge from the bleakest situations. We are empowered when we realize we have choices in responding to undesired injuries. Our wounds can become our ability to relate and minister to other people. When you have walked down a path of healing, you will frequently have the privilege of sharing it with someone else. Pain can become a chisel that makes us more like Jesus. Giving God access to our suffering can become a window in which His restoration enters.

Questions:

1) What injuries and setbacks have you experienced?
2) How can you support someone who has been deeply hurt?
3) What are some of the practical ways Jesus heals people?

Deeper Study:

Romans 12:17-21. Do what you can to live at peace with everyone.

Hebrews 13:15-18. Respect and share with those in need.

Psalm 133. The Lord's blessing is on His people who are willing to unite.

Lamentations 3:21-26. God's mercy is new today; His compassion never fails.

Prayer:

Holy God, You have made it so clear in Your Word that You want love to prevail in our relationships. May Your desires become our desires. Your will be done, not ours. Help me to be a humble person of understanding and healing. Guide me in steps of restoration. I pray this in Your powerful name, Jesus. Amen.

16) MAKING SENSE OUT OF YOUR PAST

Passage: Genesis 50:20

[Joseph said,] "You intended to harm me, but God intended it for good, to accomplish what is now being done, the saving of many lives."

Insight:

Joyce Meyer speaks worldwide today encouraging millions of people. As a child, she was frequently sexually abused by her alcoholic father.[5] Joyce never forgot what her father did to her, but she has chosen to forgive him with the help of Jesus. God helped Joyce not only to forgive her father but also to show him kindness. Joyce cared for her dad later in his life and was able to lead him to Jesus before his death. Can you imagine how she felt during those moments? Our God chooses and heals wounded people to carry out His great work! Her dad clearly saw Jesus in Joyce and received such a wonderful, gracious love.[6]

God's grace can be hidden and later seen as we reflect on the events of our life journey. Joseph was mistreated by his family—his brothers literally sold him into slavery. Later, he was thrown in jail for a crime he never committed. God eventually rescued him and gave him a promotion. Joseph is a great example of someone who continued to walk with God through his most difficult days. Have you ever persevered when it did not feel like there was any hope? In the long run, Joseph helped people from many nations during a massive famine. Surprisingly, he also provided food for the same brothers who nearly killed him. With God's help, he was able to work through many confusing and painful issues in his past and a bright future emerged, saving the lives of many people.

Application:

Despite being abandoned by his siblings, thrown into a pit, sold into slavery, falsely accused and jailed, and receiving broken promises, Joseph didn't become bitter. In fact, he blessed the people who were cruelest towards him. Let's take a close look at some of the key principles of Joseph's life (Genesis chapters 42-50):

1) Have confidence that the promises of God will endure through every circumstance (42:1-6).
2) Trust God even if you suffer from previous pain and disappointment (42:36).
3) Overcome evil with good (43:18-24).
4) Knowing when to make the right sacrifices will pave the way to a blessed future (45:2-8).
5) Reconcile with other people whenever it's possible and healthy (45:9-15).
6) Listen closely to God (Joseph and his father Jacob followed God's promptings). You can gain God's perspective and answers during your journey (46:2-4).
7) Savor what is positive in your family relationships (46:28-30).
8) One thing that you always get to choose is your response to how other people treat you (50:15-21).

Questions:

1) How has God brought healing and grace to the pain in your life?
2) What has been the most difficult experience for you to overcome?
3) Have you ever seen God turn a negative into a positive?
4) How is God encouraging you about your future?

Deeper Study:

Philippians 3:12-16. Stay focused on the future God has for you.

John 11:1-44. Your past trials can become your testimony.

Acts 16:16-34. Trust God's plans, praise Him, and watch what He does.

Psalm 40. God can turn around any situation and deliver you.

Ruth 1:16-17. Look for someone who had a rough past and make a difference.

Prayer:

Gracious God, You know everything about my past. As I reflect on my life, I want to learn from my experiences and trials. Please help me to be like Joseph and learn how to respond in a way that honors You. I pray that You will heal some of the lingering pain, forgive my unwise decisions, remove any false guilt, and help me to look ahead with your perspective of hope and courage. I trust You will do great things in my future and will build on what I have learned. And I pray this all in Jesus' name. Amen.

17) DEALING WITH DOUBTS

Passage: Matthew 11:2-6

When John heard in prison what Christ was doing, he sent his disciples to ask him, "Are you the one who was to come, or should we expect someone else?" Jesus replied, "Go back and report to John what you hear and see: The blind receive sight, the lame walk, those who have leprosy are cured, the deaf hear, the dead are raised, and the good news is preached to the poor. Blessed is the man who does not fall away on account of me."

Insight:

My first car was a used Cutlass Cruiser station wagon with "wood" paneling on the side of the car. Who wouldn't want one of those? It ran flawlessly the first few years, but mechanical issues soon became a concern. I was adding oil almost as often as I was buying gasoline, parking on inclines so water that was trapped inside the front door could be set free after it rained, and apologizing to other drivers as my car often stalled near busy intersections. Hypothetically speaking, if your car stalls and creates a traffic jam on the highway that is mentioned on the local television news, it is probably a sign that it needs repairing. Similarly, our faith can be solid at one point in our lives but later deteriorates. Have you ever sensed that your relationship with God has stalled and needs some work under the hood? This is what happened to John the Baptist.

Can God be gracious to us in spite of our struggles with faith and doubts? John the Baptist spent his entire life serving God and pointing people to Jesus. At the end of his life when he was in prison and suffering, he began to have some doubts about his Savior. Jesus reassured John by reminding him what He has done and reviewing the evidence that Jesus is the Messiah. Jesus also listed the fulfillments of prophecy from the Book of Isaiah that contained descriptions of what the coming Messiah would do. John the Baptist was a spiritual giant, but he faltered in his faith. Jesus gently guided him back to truth.

Application:

How do you handle your doubts? Doubt has the potential to be extremely dangerous. It is one of the devil's tools to pull us away from God as he did with Adam and Eve in Genesis chapter 3. Doubts invite themselves into our minds, but it is important not to believe the deceptions or act on them. On the other hand, as we grow intellectually, we are going to come to our faith with new questions. Actually, this type of searching for truth can build up our faith effectively. Here are some helpful responses when having doubts:

1) **Go to Jesus.** When John had doubts, he asked Jesus about them. Jesus was incredibly merciful with John; He even complimented John for his faith (Matthew 11:11). Ask God your most honest and difficult questions.

2) **Go to the Word.** Make sure the teaching you hear doesn't falsely undermine and deviate from what the Bible actually says. Many people intentionally and unintentionally misinterpret the Bible. Jesus reminded John of the truth of the Scriptures in His response. There can be so-called Christian teaching that is not solid and doesn't actually come from God's Word. Watch out for savage wolves and false teachers (Acts 20:29).

3) **Go to people with faith.** Thomas had doubts in John chapter 20, but he stayed in the community of faith. There are many great books today that give the intellectual evidence for our faith and answers to difficult topics. You can ask your pastor for suggested readings and resources.

Questions:

1) What do you think are the most common spiritual doubts?
2) How would you respond to people who have these doubts?
3) What have been some of the biggest doubts you have faced in your own faith?
4) Has doubt ever positively motivated you to seek more evidence for your faith?
5) What are the different ways God responds to doubt in the Bible?

Deeper Study:

Matthew 14:22-33. Some doubts are fear-based: get rid of them.

Genesis 3:1-7. The devil tries to get us to doubt God's Word.

Jude 1:22-23. Show mercy to a doubter but also share truth.

Acts 17:11. Test all spiritual teaching to see if it's consistent with the Bible.

James 1:5-8. You can ask God for wisdom in any situation.

Mark 9:20-29. Admit your unbelief to God and start choosing to believe.

Prayer:

Gracious God, I want to build up my knowledge of Your Word and the evidence that supports my faith. When doubts creep into my thinking, I want to bring them to You and trust You more. Please help me to encourage people who are having destructive doubts with their faith. I pray this in Your mighty name Jesus. Amen.

18) WHEN THERE ARE NO ANSWERS

Passage: Habakkuk 1:12, 13

O Lord, are you not from everlasting? My God, my Holy One, we will not die…Your eyes are too pure to look on evil; you cannot tolerate wrong. Why then do you tolerate the treacherous? Why are you silent while the wicked swallow up those more righteous than themselves?

Insight:

Walking through my seminary campus one morning, I noticed many people were crying. I became curious about what had happened. I soon learned that my close friend, Wilfred, was killed by a drunk driver. I was shocked, saddened, and flooded with emotions. Needlessly, I had lost a friend. He was someone who was important in my life and also in our school community. Wilfred was from Ghana and had come to Dallas to study theology. He was one of those amazing guys who could light up the entire cafeteria with his smile. You felt closer to God just by being around the man. Do you know anyone like this? And Wilfred's great love for God was so contagious. With eagerness, he was looking forward to completing his degree and then returning to serve in his country. That dream was never realized by Wilfred. Yet to honor his life, many people have travelled to Ghana and reached out to the nation. Personally, I try not to dwell on the "what-if's." I don't understand all of the reasons for this tragedy. I mourn and with trust, in the midst of lingering questions, move forward.

God never promises that we will have all of the answers on this side of heaven. Habakkuk was a prophet in the Old Testament who asked God some difficult questions. From Habakkuk's point-of-view, God appeared to be silent, ignoring the injustice and cruelty of the Babylonians. The prophet couldn't wait any longer, and he asked God why this was happening and how long it would last. God's answers were not easy to accept. God was in the process of actually raising up the Babylonians to discipline the Israelites. God reassured Habakkuk that the Babylonians were still accountable to Him and would be punished for any wrongdoings. God can bring contentment in spite of puzzling and disappointing circumstances.

Application:

Habakkuk did not avoid the tension between the issues in his life and faith. Let's take a closer look at how he proceeded through these challenges with God:

1) **He started with a question.** It is honest, and it goes directly to God (1:2-4). After adding another question, God's reply did not make sense to Habakkuk. In fact Habakkuk became even more confused and needed further clarification. Sometimes when we seek God, His answers don't make sense to us at first, but we can keep asking questions (Habakkuk 1:12-17).

2) **He took time to process what God had said.** Look at some of God's statements in this book: they are worthy of extended reflection (Habakkuk 1:5, 2:2, 2:4, 2:14, 2:20). God is not intimidated by our raw and direct honesty.

3) **He remained dissatisfied but was constructive.** Habakkuk began to pray for God to work amongst his people because the prophet now saw the seriousness of their rebellion. Habakkuk prayed for God's mercy and for positive changes (Habakkuk 3:1-2).

4) **He learned contentment in God.** Habakkuk made a decision to praise God and relied on God's strength through the difficulties. He remembered that blessings were a gift, not a right. And he remembered who was still worthy of his praise. He could only arrive at this place spiritually because he walked through the process with God (Habakkuk 3:16-19).

Questions:

1) What question would you like to ask God?
2) Does God give any answers in the Bible that are difficult to accept?
3) What are some of the ways you can follow Habakkuk's example?
4) What prevents you from speaking honestly with God?
5) What situation would you like to see change in a positive way?

Deeper Study:

Genesis 32:22-32. There can be times in your journey when you wrestle with God.

Psalm 73. God will bring justice to arrogant people- stay close to Him.

John 16:5-13. The Holy Spirit will counsel you; be sensitive to His promptings.

Deuteronomy 29:29. Respond to what you know- some mysteries will remain.

Psalm 25. God will confide in the person who seeks and trusts the Lord.

Prayer:

Father God, many of the things I see in today's world don't make sense to me. Actually, they cause me great concern. I want to respond in a way that honors You and is positive towards the people involved. Please help me to see through Your eyes and to know Your purposes too. Thank You that I can come to You with the most grueling issues and talk with You. Open my ears that I may hear Your words and guidance. I pray in Jesus' name. Amen.

ABUNDANT GRACE

God's generosity has no limits

19) LION PILLOWS

Passage: Daniel 6:20-22

> *When he came near the den, he called to Daniel in an anguished voice, "Daniel, servant of the living God, has your God, whom you serve continually, been able to rescue you from the lions?" Daniel answered, "O king, live forever! My God sent his angel, and he shut the mouths of the lions."*

Insight:

God's abundant grace can cover us in any situation, including being thrown into a lions' den. Life has a way of thrusting us into situations we don't want or expect. Do any examples from your life come to mind? At those times, we can experience God's grace to a greater degree. Have you had to face any lions in your own life? I mentioned earlier that Laurie and I endured several miscarriages. Waiting and praying to become pregnant again with the uncertainty of the next child being born and not knowing why the earlier miscarriages happened— these were all our lions. Sometimes God leads us into a lions' den, and we don't always make it out alive. There are thousands of martyrs in the last few decades that have gone to be with the Lord. We know that there are children of ours ahead of us in heaven already. When God does shut the mouths of the lions in our lives though, it's time to celebrate and share the story. By His grace, we have been able to have three children now, and we are so thankful to God.

Daniel continued to walk with faith even when it looked like he would be killed. Because of his commitment to prayer, Daniel was thrown into the lions' den by the king as a punishment. Facing ferocious lions, Daniel's only hope was the grace of God. I like to picture Daniel grabbing the whiskers of the fiercest lion, pulling him down to the ground, and sleeping on him for the night! Then I picture Daniel asking the other lions to come close to keep him warm, and enjoying the best night of sleep in years. All we know is that Daniel emerged the next day from this death trap completely unharmed. And He was quick to give God the glory.

Application:

As we read Daniel chapter 6 and the account of his survival in the lions' den, we can glean practical lessons from this event. The lions' den became fertile grounds for a miracle. We know from Hebrews chapter 11, verse 6 that God is pleased when we seek His face and look to Him for help.

It's important to note what Daniel didn't do: complain, worry, despair, quit, slander, or pout. If we are honest, these are all very tempting options when we are mistreated or thrown into a pack of hungry lions. Sometimes, it's what we choose not to do that creates room for the good things that God wants to give us.

Even in a lions' den, Daniel wasn't completely trapped. He was able to make four important decisions in the midst of his challenges:

1) Daniel chose to not let anyone or anything stop him from praying to God!
2) Daniel chose to live out his faith and be courageous even when it meant he would suffer for God.
3) Daniel chose to take no glory for the works of God in his life.

4) Daniel chose to let other people know about the goodness of the Lord.

Questions:

1) Have there been times in your life when you had to face your fears?
2) What has God rescued you from in your journey?
3) What are the reasons God does miracles?
4) When was the last time God exceeded your expectations?
5) What comfort is there in the middle of a lions' den?

Deeper Study:

Ephesians 3:20-21. You can't put limits on what God can accomplish.

Psalm 115:1. God deserves the credit for what He alone can do.

Luke 1:34-38. Jesus' birth reminds us of God's supernatural abilities.

Psalm 103:1-5. It's good to recall your blessings from God and proclaim it.

Psalm 91:11-13. God sends angels to protect you in danger.

Hebrews 13:3. Remember to pray for those who are persecuted or in prison.

Prayer:

Almighty God, I know there are times in my life when I will be facing lions. Help me not to worry or be afraid. May my trust in You increase and my wavering commitment to You become solid. When You rescue me Lord, help me give You the glory You deserve. And when You want to be glorified through what appears to be a tragedy, may I bless Your name then too. I pray for this in Your strength, Jesus. Amen.

20) HOPE FOR A NATION

Passage: Habakkuk 3:2

> *Lord, I have heard of your fame; I stand in awe of your deeds, O Lord. Renew them in our day, in our time make them known; in wrath remember mercy.*

Insight:

September 11, 2001 was a day etched in our memories as Americans because of the immense sadness we endured. I have never seen something so horrific, and I have never seen so many people come streaming into the church to pray. What followed the tragic loss of lives was powerful! There was a greater expression of community in our nation, a willingness to help those who were suffering and mourning, a sense of deep unity, and an increase in prayer. We had been attacked in a vicious way and were wondering how our nation could recover. I realize that many people in America then and today don't believe in God. But I saw many people turning to the overflowing grace of God in the days that followed that tragedy. As the Bible reminds us; God is our refuge, strength, and an ever-present help in trouble (Psalm 46). We can receive His comfort and perseverance both as individuals and as a country.

God's grace allows us to take positive steps forward when we are tempted to be discouraged. Instead of complaining about the situation, God wants us to be part of the solution. Sometimes we are asked to step up and make a difference on a national level. Be careful not to write off any person or country—God is merciful and doesn't stop His good work. What would you like to see happen in your country? Habakkuk was a prophet who lived 600 years before Jesus. He wrestled with the same questions we face today: why is there so much evil? How long until things change? Will God demonstrate His power in this generation? The first two chapters of Habakkuk cover an incredible conversation between the prophet and God. Habakkuk knew he could pour out his soul in the most honest way with God. His intense questions led him to prayer and eventually to God's plentiful grace.

There are three qualities that emerge in Habakkuk's prayer:

1) **Humility:** "Lord, I have heard of your fame; I stand in awe of your deeds, O Lord." Habakkuk gave God his full respect because of who God is and what God has done.

2) **Desire:** "Renew them in our day, in our time make them known;" Habakkuk had an intense hunger for God to do something in his generation. He wanted to see God's glory.

3) **Confession:** "In wrath, remember mercy." Habakkuk pleaded with God to have mercy and to forgive rebellion. He prayed that hearts would change and nations would turn to God in prayer. His plea was based on the kindness of God.

Application:

Jeremiah Lanphier began a prayer meeting in 1857 in New York City. It was during the lunch hour, and only a few people joined him in prayer. They continued every week and before long, people began to respond. Within six months, ten thousand business people were gathering in prayer in New York City. Other prayer meetings started in the city in the middle of the day. Soon, there were thousands of people praying in cities such as Pittsburgh and Washington D.C. This was the catalyst for The Great Awakening from 1857-1860, in which it was estimated that over a million people came to know Jesus. The revival extended into many other countries too. Jeremiah Lanphier and his friends felt the burden to begin to pray for their country and took the initiative to ask other people to join them in seeking God.[7]

Questions:

1) Do you believe prayer can make a difference in your country?
2) What changes or spiritual awakening would you like to see happen?
3) What does it mean to ask God to heal our land?
4) What do humility, desire, and confession look like in your prayer times?

Deeper Study:

Psalm 96. You have a role in the spiritual health of your nation.

Daniel 9:1-19. Genuine repentance can change a country.

Nehemiah 1:1-11. Let God direct your work and bring His favor to your individual role.

Jonah 3:1-10. Seeking God brings blessing and fruit.

1 Timothy 2:1-4. Pray for the leaders in your country.

2 Chronicles 7:14. There is true hope for any nation that seeks God.

Prayer:

Father God, You are able to do all things. I don't want to be discouraged when I see challenges in our country. I want to pray more and complain less. Help me to live what I say I believe and to take action. Our country needs You now, Lord. I ask that You will bring a spiritual awakening. Please have mercy, bring healing, and forgive us, I pray in Jesus' name. Amen.

21)   HOW TO HANDLE A BLESSING

Passage: Genesis 37:3-7

> *Now Israel [Jacob] loved Joseph more than any of his other sons, because he had been born to him in his old age; and he made a richly ornamented robe for him. When his brothers saw that their father loved him more than any of them, they hated him [Joseph] and could not speak a kind word to him. Joseph had a dream, and when he told it to his brothers, they hated him all the more. He said to them, "Listen to this dream I had: We were binding sheaves of grain out in the field when suddenly my sheaf rose and stood upright, while your sheaves gathered around mine and bowed down to it."*

Insight:

Jacob, also called Israel, had many sons, but he didn't love them equally. Do you think it helped family unity when he expressed it? This is the story of how a dad's preferences led to some very unhealthy family dynamics. There is some humor in this story as you think about sibling rivalries. Can you imagine the youngest brother going up to his older brothers and telling them that they are going to be bowing down to him? Are they going to think that this is a fantastic idea? God's favor was on Jacob in his old age and Joseph from an early age in life, but neither of them knew how to handle blessings and success.

Abundant grace is so desirable, but it can also lead to a new set of decisions. Success can bring unexpected challenges that fly under your radar, and God's favor and grace can be mishandled. It can be difficult to receive from the Lord and stay humble. Ironically, your success can potentially become a stumbling block in your faith. Has success been easy for you to handle? Recognizing that God is the giver of every good thing in your life will help protect your humility. Your health, motivation, ability, and opportunities are truly from His hand.

Application:

There are four ways to mishandle a blessing that we read about in Genesis chapter 37:

1) **Unfaithfulness:** Jacob's children were so blessed to have a father who was a godly man. They probably took their blessings for granted and felt a sense of entitlement. They learned that they were not above accountability, though, when their father received a bad report about their behavior (Genesis 37:1-2).

2) **Favoritism:** God gave Jacob a son in his old age, and Jacob was so appreciative of this gift. But Jacob didn't realize how much he showed favoritism to Joseph which made his other kids feel like second-class children. We can get caught up in our preferences and desires resulting in foolish decisions (Genesis 37: 3-4).

3) **Careless Words:** Just because you are excited about something or have an idea, it may not be wise to talk about it. This is difficult for extroverts. Joseph is giddy about his dream, but he loses all discretion and tact. He blurts out what he wants to say instead of considering how God wants him to react (Genesis 37:5-8).

4) **Pride:** Have you ever made a mistake and then repeated it again a short time later? Joseph apparently didn't learn from his interaction with his brothers because he acted the same way with his parents too. His blessings had gone to his head (Genesis 37:9-11).

Here is God's wisdom for when blessings come into your life. These principles are found in Genesis 37:12-36:

1) Protect blessings from jealous rivals.
2) Look for the subtle blessings during barren times.
3) Remember that God can use unlikely connections to deliver blessings.
4) Don't be discouraged—crooked people don't stay ahead.

5) God is often working on your promotion behind the scenes.

Questions:

1) Have you stopped and thanked God recently for His blessings and provision?
2) Have you ever mishandled a blessing?
3) Have you ever realized God was working behind the scenes?
4) How can you stay humble when you are given blessings?

Deeper Study:

1 Thessalonians 5:16-24. God's will for you is to give thanks in all circumstances.

Luke 17:11-19. Be someone who doesn't take Jesus and His gifts for granted.

1 Peter 5:5-11. If you are humble, God will exalt you.

James 1:16-18. God is the source of every blessing in your life.

Prayer:

Father God, thank You for the new blessings You bring everyday. Please help me to walk humbly with You. I realize that Jesus' death and resurrection are the only reasons I can be forgiven and go to heaven. Let me never forget all that You have done for me. I want to be a grateful person and notice Your hand even in the difficult times. Thank You for blessing me with Your presence even more than your presents. And I pray this all in Jesus' name. Amen.

22)   UNRIVALED JESUS

Passage: Matthew 16:13-16

When Jesus came to the region of Caesarea Philippi, he asked his disciples, "Who do people say the Son of Man is?" They replied, "Some say John the Baptist; others say Elijah; and still others, Jeremiah or one of the prophets." But what about you?" he asked. "Who do you say I am?" Simon Peter answered, "You are the Christ, the Son of the living God."

Insight:

When I took my first religion course at Dartmouth College, I found it interesting because the professor was critical of the Bible. I wasn't a Christian at the time, but his approach made me curious, and I decided to read the Bible for the first time. As a child, I enjoyed Christmas because of the presents and Easter for the candy and the egg hunts. But I had never really thought about Jesus deeply before the class. When was the first time you heard about Jesus? What was your initial reaction? When I began to study the different religious leaders, Jesus sparked my interest because He is so unique. As I was gaining information, I realized that I would need to make some decisions about what I believe.

The grace of Jesus caught my attention because there is simply no one like Him. Jesus knows who He is, but He asks a series of questions so that His disciples will realize who He is and put their trust in Him. John the Baptist, Elijah, and Jeremiah were significant religious leaders, but Jesus is in a different category.

What makes Jesus unique?

1)   Jesus has more followers than any other religious leader.

2) Even many atheists agree that Jesus is the greatest teacher of all time.

3) Jesus is the only person who has not sinned.

4) His list of miracles include calming storms, healing the sick and blind, walking on water, casting out demons, and raising dead people to life.

5) His prophetic statements have all proven to be true in incredible detail.

6) Jesus paid the full price for our sins through His sacrificial death on a cross.

7) Jesus is the only religious leader with an empty tomb—He is risen!

8) He is both fully human and fully God at the same time.

9) He was born through a virgin, Mary, as predicted in the Bible.

10) Jesus claims to be the Messiah, God's Son.

Application:

How do we respond to Jesus and His overflowing grace? The famous author C.S. Lewis made a profound insight: he pointed out that when someone claims to be the Son of God and the Messiah, there are only three possible conclusions to choose from: 1) He is a liar because he knows it is not true. 2) He is a lunatic because he believes he really is the Savior of the world, but in reality he is not the One. 3) He really is the Lord and Messiah. There have been many people who claimed to be the Messiah throughout history, but Jesus backed up His claims with tremendous amounts of evidence. When Jesus claims to be God, He can no longer be just a nice guy and a good teacher! We now only have three options to choose from: liar, lunatic, or the Lord.[8] We can't decide to follow Jesus without receiving His abundant grace.

Questions:

1) Which unique quality of Jesus stands out to you the most?
2) Is there anything preventing you from putting your trust in Jesus or fully following Him?
3) How have you studied Jesus' life and come to your conclusions about Him?
4) In what ways are you drawn to follow Jesus and grow in your faith?

Deeper Study:

Mark 2:1-12. Jesus has the ability to forgive sins because He is God.

John 5:39-40. Someone can study Scripture but not have a relationship with Jesus.

John 6:66-69. You need to decide for yourself if you really want to follow Jesus.

Revelation 5:9-14. People from every nation will praise Jesus in heaven.

Prayer:

God, thank You for all of the ways that Jesus is unique. I want to walk closer with You Lord. I confess I often underestimate You. Forgive me for the times I deny You. Help me to see You clearer and to live for You, and I pray this in Your name, Lord. Amen.

23)   CHARACTER IN A CRISIS

Passage: Genesis 39:7-10

His master's wife took notice of Joseph and said, "Come to bed with me!"' But he refused... "How then could I do such a wicked thing and sin against God?" And though she spoke to Joseph day after day, he refused to go to bed with her or even be with her.

Insight:

A crisis doesn't confine God; in fact, it can set the stage for His grace to shine. The abundant grace of God can help us respond in a godly way in any situation. No, you aren't experiencing déjà vu as you read this chapter: I previously covered an overview of Joseph's life in this book. Let's now focus on some specifics from his journey. The life of Joseph contains so many reminders that God's grace is very practical in our relationships and in the moments when we are at a crossroad in life. Have you faced any situations where you knew that your decision would have massive implications for the rest of your life?

Joseph lived in Egypt and worked for Potiphar when Potiphar's wife demanded that he sleep with her. Joseph knew it would be a sin against God, and he was able to refuse her. Because he was reflecting on how abundantly gracious God had been to him, there was a strong, grace-driven motive to choose purity. After Joseph denied her request, she had him thrown in prison. It's one thing to say we follow God, but what really matters is what we decide to do in a crisis. Joseph risked losing his job, place to live, money, freedom, and even his life as he maintained his integrity. He didn't choose this problem, but he stayed committed to follow God in the midst of it.

Application:

Let's take a look at some of the principles Joseph lived by in Genesis chapter 39:

1) **Stay alert because success can lull you to sleep: a crisis can be just around the corner.** Things were going well in Joseph's job, but he stayed alert and handled the new problem with courage and wisdom.

2) **One inviting person and one slippery moment can threaten what is most dear to you.** When someone asks you to do something, always check in with God before you say yes.

3) **Be able to give a firm refusal.** When you know it is right to say no to an offer, be stubborn about not entertaining the idea. Hold your ground.

4) **Speak openly about your faith.** Let others know that you don't want to sin against God and you want to follow Him.

5) **Call sin what it really is.** Don't try to make it sound like it's no big deal or fine because everyone is doing it— that is just an excuse.

6) **Doing the right thing is the best thing.** You will have peace of mind when you act with integrity. Leave the results up to God.

7) **Don't linger when it's time to run.** With some temptations the wise thing to do is to run and leave the situation quickly.

8) **God's anointing gets stronger with good decisions.** The Holy Spirit fills you more when you honor Him.

9) **There might be times when God is all you have, and that's okay, He is enough.** If there is opposition to your godly decisions, God will still be there with you to sustain you.

Questions:

1) How do you make good decisions in a crisis?

2) Which of the principles above is most helpful to you now?

3) Have you ever done the right thing when it wasn't popular?

Deeper Study:

2 Timothy 2:22-26. God will help you walk in purity and gently speak the truth.

James 3:13-18. Receive the wisdom that comes from heaven.

Galatians 5:22-26. Give the Holy Spirit full access to your life and see the results.

Job 2:7-10. Hold on to your faith even if people criticize it.

Proverbs 10:9. When you walk in integrity, you will be secure.

Prayer:

God of all wisdom, thank You for examples like Joseph. Help me to be someone who will live out my faith in difficult situations. Even if I'm outnumbered, I want to stay faithful to You. I want to be a light in dark places. I pray this all in Your name, Jesus. Amen.

24)   COURAGEOUS TRANSPARENCY

Passage: Psalm 139: 1-4

O Lord, you have searched me and you know me. You know when I sit and when I rise; you perceive my thoughts from afar. You discern my going out and my lying down; you are familiar with all my ways. Before a word is on my tongue you know it completely, O Lord.

Insight:

I woke up one morning and decided to wear a T-shirt as an undershirt. There was writing and a design on the shirt, but it was not visible to the human eye because I had a dark-colored sweater over it. I forgot about the T-shirt until I walked in front of a security camera. The screen that was linked to the camera showed the design of my T-shirt. The camera made visible what I thought was hidden! It startled me, and it was a little unnerving. Have you ever thought something was private only to learn that it was actually very evident to other people? Fortunately, the picture on my T-shirt that appeared was just the wings of an eagle, so there was no reason to be embarrassed. The experience made me think about how God can see through anything, and nothing is hidden before Him.

Why do we try to hide parts of our lives from God? Living in Dallas, Texas, for four years introduced me to supersized cockroaches. Yes, one of these bugs literally woke me up one night as it was having a good time exploring my garbage can. On another occasion, I grabbed my phone early in the morning, without looking first, and I felt a cockroach slither out from underneath my hand. Have you ever touched one? I don't recommend it. My immediate reaction was to turn on my lamp. The cockroach climbed underneath my bookshelf, preferring the darkness. Strangely, this incident became a spiritual metaphor for me. My cockroach encounter was a visible reminder that God calls us out of darkness and helps us run to His marvelous light. I don't want to live like a cockroach!

Do you ever try to put limits on God by attempting to keep certain parts of your life private from Him? David wrote this psalm as he came to grips with the truth that all thoughts, all actions, all habits, all preferences, and all words are visible and known to God all of the time. This is a reality we often ignore. It is both comforting and uncomfortable at the same time. It is comforting because there is One who really understands and loves us! It can be humbling though to know that none of our actions or thoughts can be hidden. Ultimately, this combination is what makes us appreciate how abundant God's mercy and grace truly is. Recognizing the depth and totality of His grace produces a wonderful security for our souls. We can begin to live in true freedom which includes the desire to please the One who has brought us real love. Underneath our fears, we realize that we are both fully known and also fully accepted by God, thanks to Jesus and His sacrifice on our behalf.

Application:

Transparency can be a complicated topic. Is transparency good? Who can you trust? What are the benefits of being open and honest? I have been on retreats and at camps where people begin to open up and share things about their lives they had never shared before. As a listener, you realize that it is a privilege to be included in their confidences. If it is done well, the one who shares can experience a release of burdens and begin a deep healing. There can be significant spiritual insights and positive life choices made when the environment is supportive.

Here are some important things to keep in mind about opening up:

1) Before you start sharing make sure the setting is appropriate and the listeners can be trusted. Don't give

gossips and dangerous people too much access to your life.

2) It will be scary to share the more destructive choices you make. We often stay private because we don't want to change; sinful habits don't survive very well in the light. It's often said that revealing is the first step toward healing.

3) It may help you to first write down the things you have kept hidden. Pray about what to do with the information. Consider who in your life is safe to talk to. Be courageous when the listener and timing is right.

4) Remember how God views you and find security in it. Before you talk with anyone else, know that Jesus wants to extend His grace to you. Let that sink in before and after you talk to someone.

Questions:

1) Are there any parts of your life that you are trying to hide from God?

2) What areas of your life can you begin to start sharing with God?

3) Is there anything that would be good to tell someone?

4) When is privacy a good thing?

Deeper Study:

Psalm 62. It is good to pour your heart out to God in prayer.

Psalm 32. An honest relationship with God includes deep confession.

1 Corinthians 14:24-25. Nothing is hidden from God; His presence reveals us.

James 5:16. It is healing to admit mistakes and yet still receive God's love.

3 John 1:2-4. A healthy soul is even more important than a healthy body.

Prayer:

Gracious God, I'm so glad that You know me fully and still love me. I find my security in You and Your acceptance of me. And it gives me courage to be more open and honest with people I can trust. I want to be authentic and not live a double life. I want to be a Christian who has integrity before You and other people. I pray for Your help in Jesus' name. Amen.

RELATIONAL GRACE

God's love can be visible in our interactions

25) PRAYING FOR UNITY

Passage: John 17:22-23

> *[Jesus prayed] "I have given them the glory that you gave me, that they may be one as we are one: I in them and you in me. May they be brought to complete unity to let the world know that you sent me and have loved them even as you have loved me."*

Insight:

It wasn't easy to organize, but one of my most satisfying memories of serving Jesus in Iowa was gathering together people from across the state to pray and worship together in unity. Have you ever experienced unity between groups of people who don't naturally come together? The gathering occurred because God prompted us to dream about unity across the entire state. Even though everyone had full schedules, we stopped our normal activities for one day to travel and seek God together. There were relational bridges built that day that continue to be strong. The event became an annual tradition because on those days of unity we tasted the sweetness of true fellowship.

Unity flourishes when there is a foundation of grace and truth. Jesus' longest prayer in the Bible is found in John chapter 17. The emphasis of our Savior's prayer is the topic of unity. Here are a few clear principles that emerge from this chapter:

1) **Jesus prays passionately for our unity**. As you read Jesus' prayer in John chapter 17, notice how many times that Jesus highlights and pleads for oneness amongst His followers.

2) **The standard for unity is found in the relationships within the Trinity.** There is one God as three divine persons, the Father, the Son, and the Holy Spirit. Reading John chapters 14-16 helps us discover the love, submission, shared purpose, obedience, and humility that are all essential parts of true unity and are completed in the Father, Son, and Holy Spirit.

3) **We have a responsibility to maintain a unity that honors God.** Unity is not just a good idea; it's something that God wants us to make every effort to keep. Listen to God's heart on this topic of unity and imitate Him.

Application:

Have you ever thought about how and why unity breaks down? Have you ever been disappointed as your hopes for unity are crushed? There are many pitfalls on the road to achieving a healthy unity. With God's help we need to be able to rise above some of the common challenges that hinder our progress.

One of the major stumbling blocks is pride. Pride has a way of sneaking into your heart, home and church. But once it takes hold, it's hardly subtle. Proverbs 13:10 says, "Pride only breeds quarrels". Proverbs 11:2 instructs, "When pride comes, then comes disgrace, but with humility comes wisdom". You won't achieve a level of unity that surpasses your level of humility. With that in mind, repentance usually precedes unity because there is a need to drop selfish pride.

Another significant obstacle to unity is a critical spirit (people who have a bent towards perfectionism need to be careful here). A spouse can feel the brunt of constant correcting. It grieves me when I hear a Christian mocking the style of another church just because it's different or is not their personal preference. Sometimes it sounds like churches are even competing against each other. This is not from God. When churchgoers criticize music styles, volumes, lights, instruments, technology, songs and hymns, body posture in worship, and so on, a church isn't second rate because of its choices in those areas. Scripture brings clarity regarding major Christian doctrinal statements, and unity regarding the essentials is important. But where the Bible gives freedom, we need to be careful not to judge or to make comments that tear down other people and ministries with reckless words.

Unforgiveness destroys unity. We can't be bitter and united at the same time. If we have been hurt, healing is often a process that begins by forgiving first. But the Bible says that forgiveness needs to be immediate and complete. Because Jesus paid the price for all of our sins, we need to fully forgive anyone who has wronged us (Matthew 18:21-35). We need to let go of grudges and all attempts at revenge. Don't give the enemy a foothold in your life, but choose to forgive even if someone doesn't deserve it. Get rid of bitterness for Jesus' glory and our own spiritual, mental, and physical health.

Questions:

1) How would you explain the unity that Jesus describes?
2) Can you initiate peace in any of your relationships through forgiveness?
3) What do you learn about unity from relationships within the Trinity?

Deeper Study:

Philemon 1:1-25. You might have the opportunity to restore someone.

Amos 3:3. God desires that we walk together in a common purpose.

Genesis 50:18-21. Forgiveness is a vital step toward unity.

Daniel 3:1-30. Find people who will agree with you in prayer and persevere.

Prayer:

Father God, thank You for helping us to see what hinders unity. It's not always natural for us to choose unity. Forgive us for how we treat each other. People will see You in us when we really love each other. Let us step up to this challenge and be intentional about building bridges of unity and grace. May it start with us. I pray this in Your great name, Jesus. Amen.

26)   TRUE FORGIVENESS

Passage: Ephesians 4:31-32

Get rid of all bitterness, rage and anger, brawling and slander, along with every form of malice. Be kind and compassionate to one another, forgiving each other, just as in Christ God forgave you.

Insight:

I once attended the funeral of a man who was shot and killed for no reason, other than the shooter had wanted to impress his friends. Have you seen any tragedies that shook you to the core? What transpired next was remarkably inspiring. Watching the parents of the victim communicate forgiveness to a watching city was life changing. It was perfectly clear that Jesus was giving them this ability in the middle of their loss. Mourning was not minimized in any way, but there was a sincere expression of forgiveness and grace in spite of such a cruel attack. How would you respond if your son was murdered? God can relate to that level of pain. From the cross, Jesus asked His Father to forgive the people who killed Him. The gift of forgiveness was demonstrated by Jesus when He died on the cross to forgive you.

As you walk through relational grace, perhaps the greatest expression of your faith is a consistent loving forgiveness. So what does forgiveness look like in a relationship? Forgiveness is a decision in which you choose not to hold anything against someone. The other person may not deserve to be forgiven, but you give it as a gift. It is the decision to let go of any grudges, bitterness, or any attempt to get even. God is very clear that vengeance is His and His alone. Forgiveness can be a very difficult choice especially when you have been hurt deeply. It is also a decision that you may need to make over and over again. You might even need to forgive the same person many times in one day. But it is always the best decision. Otherwise you can get trapped in negative thoughts and actions and carry anger with you for months or years. Bitterness can trap and eventually destroy you, so don't harbor it. Relational grace through forgiveness to others can also set you free.

Application:

What does God mean when He tells you to forgive someone?

1) **Forgiveness does not mean that we forget.** Don't feel guilty if you remember the specific words or actions in which someone hurt you. The memories don't always fade.

2) **Forgiveness can be different than the healing process.** God can bring healing in many ways, but healing is often a process that can take a long time. Forgiveness, though, is a decision that should be done right away.

3) **Forgiveness can include distance.** It may be healthy to have some space or distance from the person who hurt you, so they don't continue to do more damage. Different types of boundaries can be a helpful for your protection.

4) **Forgiveness is more than a suggestion.** God says you need to forgive people just as Christ has forgiven you. This is for your own good, and it glorifies God too.

The Ability To Forgive

How do you find the power to forgive? It comes from Jesus. You can start by thinking about the cross and how Jesus paid the price for your sins. God has given you eternal and complete forgiveness through Jesus. After receiving this gift, now you need to offer that same forgiveness to other people. There have been many people in my life whom I couldn't forgive until I came to know Jesus. Experiencing forgiveness from God carries over into your relationships with other people. Look over what the Bible says about forgiveness. Make your decision to forgive everyone who has hurt you. Both you and the people you forgive will benefit as you extend grace. This will also accelerate the healing process in your life.

Questions:

1) Why is it important to realize that forgiveness is a choice?
2) Is there anyone you still need to forgive?
3) What has brought healing into your life when you have been hurt?
4) How does forgiving people bring glory to God?

Deeper Study:

Matthew 6:12-15. God expects you to forgive everyone fully.

Matthew 18:15-20. Make the decision to forgive just as God has forgiven you.

1 Peter 3:8-9. Your calling is to live in harmony and with compassion.

Mark 11:22-25. Forgive other people so that your prayers will be heard.

Prayer:

Gracious God, thank You that Your forgiveness is real and complete in Jesus. I accept and thank You for your mercy towards me. I want to pass this gift on to other people by forgiving other people who hurt me. I know You have something better than bitterness for my life. I choose to walk in freedom and let You handle all vengeance. I commit this to You in Jesus' name. Amen.

27)   HOW TO GIVE OR RECEIVE A REBUKE

Passage: Proverbs 9:8 and 27:5

> *Do not rebuke a mocker or he will hate you; rebuke a wise man and he will love you. Better is open rebuke than hidden love.*

Insight:

While my wife and I were dating we encountered some significant conflicts in our relationship, especially during our engagement period. I did what everyone wants to do when having an argument: go find a friend who would take sides with me. I just knew Doug would back my claims and would completely affirm my perspective. I laid out to him what had happened, what was said, reactions, reasons, and what the resolution should look like. But there was silence. Sometimes silence can be a good rebuke all by itself. Then Doug added a few words, "Jesse, I think there are some ways that you can improve on how you lead and handle this situation." That was not the advice I was looking for, but it was exactly what I needed to hear! Have your friends ever done something like this to you? Good friends know how and when to challenge you and help you reach the next level in your relationships and your faith.

A friend can be honest and gracious at the same time. A good rebuke is given when you truly care about someone else; it's vital in friendships. God's grace produces the courage needed to give a rebuke and the humility to receive one. Have you been in a situation where you saw something that wasn't right, and you needed to speak up? The Bible gives you some practical advice about when and how to address an issue. If rebukes are done in a sloppy or spiteful manner, they can be dangerous in relationships. It's important to look to God's Word as you live out these situations. Rebukes are actually God's design, emerging from love. Jesus says He rebukes those He loves

(Revelation 3:19). For many people, this topic is an area of needed growth. Receiving a rebuke can hurt initially, but it will be a great gift to your character.

Application:

Here are seven practical steps when you consider rebuking someone:

1) **Praying first before speaking can avoid some wrong turns.** Be careful not to just rush into a rebuke; connect with God beforehand. Also, let your tone and words be sincere and kind (Proverbs 25:12).

2) **Don't let the issue fester inside of you.** The Bible says don't let the sun go down on your anger (Ephesians 4:26). Nothing good will come from nursing a grudge.

3) **Make sure you have the actual facts.** It's important that what you are saying is accurate. Rumors aren't reliable. Accusations that are off base can be very damaging.

4) **Writing something down can help you clarify the situation.** In the heat of the moment, you can forget a thought, ramble on, or say something you later regret. Taking time to write things down can solve some of these issues (Ecclesiastes 7:5).

5) **Calmly explain your perspective, and don't exaggerate or be negative.** Be humble at all times. Even if you feel strongly about an issue, don't let your emotions take control.

6) **A rebuke gives an opportunity to set someone free.** If we never rebuke each other, we maintain destructive patterns. Rebukes are not easy to give or receive. They usually don't feel good. Be capable of doing something that is needed even if it is difficult. We need each other to be honest, so we can grow and make positive changes.

Here are some practical steps when you are rebuked by someone:

1) **Kindly repeat what you have heard and ask the other person if you have heard them correctly.** This will clear up any misunderstandings and also give you a minute to take a deep breath (Proverbs 15:31).

2) **Is there any validity to the rebuke?** Don't let your pride get in the way of some area in your life that you can grow spiritually or in your character (Proverbs 3:11).

3) **Is there a blind spot or is it stubbornness?** There is a difference between not realizing the harmful things you are doing and knowing what is right but refusing to do it (Psalm 141:5).

4) **Find out what help is available for deeper issues.** There are many people who love you and would like to help you in your struggles. Don't isolate yourself. Professional counselors are equipped to help and can be a good option. Pastors can be helpful too!

5) **Stay out of unhealthy sorrow.** Don't beat yourself up or be too hard on yourself. God doesn't want you to wallow in guilt and shame. Turn to Him for His mercy and grace and accept it. Don't just feel bad about the consequences; have a change of heart and find a new way to walk with Jesus.

Questions:

1) When was the last time you gave or received a rebuke?
2) What did you learn from the experience?
3) Do you need more sensitivity when you speak the truth?
4) What are some reasons that rebukes are good?

Deeper Study:

2 Corinthians 7:8-12. The goal of a rebuke is not a "guilt trip"; it is repentance.

Hosea 6:1-3. An honest rebuke is frequently an invitation to return to God.

Leviticus 19:16-18. A good rebuke comes out of a heart of love and concern.

Ephesians 4:15. Don't withhold the truth because you are afraid of someone's reaction.

Prayer:

Father God, it can be so difficult to rebuke someone. Please help me to have the courage to do it tactfully and to choose my words and tone wisely. I want to be an instrument of Your love, to bring Your healing, guidance, wisdom, and grace to others. It can be so difficult to be rebuked too. Please help me to have the humility to receive it well. I know that rebukes are a gift You use to make me more like You. Please help me to be discerning when other people rebuke me, so that I hear Your voice clearly. I pray this all in Your name, Jesus. Amen.

28)   WHAT ONE TONGUE CAN DO

Passage: James 3:9-10

> *With the tongue we praise our Lord and Father, and with it we curse men, who have been made in God's likeness. Out of the same mouth come praise and cursing. My brothers, this should not be.*

Insight:

It's been said that the most difficult parts of our lives to come under the Lordship of Jesus are: the right foot that we use to step on the gas pedal, the attitude we carry during athletic competition, and the tongue we use to speak during the week. If we want to live a life of grace, then let God transform the way we talk to and about people. This includes when they are in the room with us and when they are miles away from our voice.

When I was in preschool, my teacher invited both my mother and me to her house. What began as a special visit was instantly transformed into a very awkward moment. Like most children my age, I simply voiced my thought as I proclaimed, "This place is a mess!" My mother could not think of anything to say in the long silence that followed my observation. Even though we have laughed about my comment many times, that day was an undesirable start to a friendship. Fortunately, the three of us are still very close many years after our initial visit.

The real freedom of speech is not the right to say anything we want to say. Freedom of speech is deeper than that: it's the power to not say cruel things, and the ability to choose a positive, greater purpose in the words and tone we use. In the verses above, James is highlighting the fact that glorious words can come out of our mouth, and then a few hours later, some wretched statements come out of that same mouth. No person can tame their tongue on their own, but with God's help our words can bring Him glory and encourage others.

Application:

1) **There is accountability for our words.** Check out what Jesus said in Matthew 12:33-36; Jesus doesn't want us to be careless with our words.

2) **God has given our words incredible power to influence lives.** Solomon tells us in Proverbs 18:21 that the power of life and death are in the tongue.

3) **We need to rely on God everyday for the right words.** This is David's prayer in Psalm 19-God can help us choose the right words to speak.

A Few Things To Avoid:

1) **Over-involved comments:** The Bible literally tells us to mind our own business, staying out of areas that are not our responsibility (1 Thessalonians 4:11).

2) **Serving hands and a wrecking ball mouth:** Some people who make the most poisonous comments are sometimes those who serve. True servants have both humble mouths and helpful hands.

3) **False flattery:** Don't sweet-talk people or be so intimidated that you can't be honest (Psalm 12:2).

4) **Sneaky private conversations:** Some people give themselves special permission to gossip and slander when they are with others. The truth is they are not alone—God hears everything.

Helpful Suggestions:

1) Before you speak, ask yourself these questions: Is it true? Is this the best way to say it?

2) Take time to think who needs your affirmation- how can you strengthen other people with words?

3) Thank the people who encourage your faith. You can initiate conversations that spread the grace of Jesus.

Questions:

1) Has someone said something so positive to you that you will never forget it?
2) Why does God give such power to our tongues?
3) How does God help you filter your words in an effective way?

Deeper Study:

Isaiah 50:4. My words can sustain weary people.

Proverbs 26:28. False flattery is a form of deception.

Proverbs 28:23. In the long run, people will respect our helpful rebukes.

James 3:1-12. Life and death are wrapped up in the tongue.

Prayer:

Father God, I want to thank You for giving me the ability to make a difference in this world with the words I speak. Forgive me for tearing other people down, being judgmental, and missing opportunities to tell people about You. I choose today to devote my words to Your purpose, and I ask Your help in beginning to speak in a new way. I want my words to bring life and lead many to You. I pray this in Your name, Jesus. Amen.

29) RADICAL GENEROSITY

Passage: Luke 8:1-3

> *After this, Jesus traveled about from one town and village to another, proclaiming the good news of the kingdom of God. The Twelve were with him, and also some women who had been cured of evil spirits and diseases: Mary (called Magdalene) from whom seven demons had come out; Joanna the wife of Cuza, the manager of Herod's household; Susanna; and many others. These women were helping to support them out of their own means.*

Insight:

All of the profits from the purchase of this book go directly to Compassion International®, an organization that is releasing children from poverty. Compassion International® sponsors over 1.2 million children in 26 countries.[9] One of their prayers is that these numbers would triple in the near future. As we put our children to bed at night, we pray with them for children who don't have beds, medical care, or enough food to survive. God is using Compassion International® to spread the grace of Jesus around the world.

Even though Jesus created everything in the world, He still relies on other people to support His ministry financially. Why would He do this? It is a demonstration of His humility. But more important, it gives people the opportunity to participate in His ministry in a tangible way. The women who supported Jesus in this passage gave with grateful hearts. They truly wanted to give back to the One who healed and rescued them. And they could see how their financial gifts were being used to reach other people. God wants His grace to flow through all of our relationships. There was a deep conviction that the best investment of their money was to support Jesus. Our time, energy, and finances are just a few ways for us to display His relational grace. God's pure joy comes to those who are generous.

Application:

Joanna sets the example for us in this passage in terms of generous giving:

1) **It was risky.** Joanna's husband was the manager of Herod's household, and Herod was violently opposed to Jesus. If Herod found out that his money and paychecks were going to support Jesus, he would have been furious to know this fact. Ultimately, Joanna was risking her life to give financially to Jesus. She also gave her time and willingness to travel as they journeyed from town to town.

2) **It was rewarded.** In Luke 24:1-10, we read about the resurrection of Jesus. After watching Jesus die on the cross (Luke 23: 44-49), Joanna was one of the first people to see Jesus appear after exiting the tomb. Jesus was risen, and He wanted Joanna to know this miracle firsthand. What a privilege! Jesus had not forgotten her generosity and service.

Opportunities:

Even a little money can go a long way—here is a list of some ideas:

1) Give a generous percentage of the money you earn to good causes.

2) Take someone out to lunch to show God's love in a practical way.

3) Make some food bags and give them out to people in need.

4) Buy a Bible for someone in a different country (www.gfa.org).

5) Surprise someone by unexpectedly paying their bill at a store.

Questions:

1) How have you used your money, time, and energy to serve God?
2) Why is generosity and risky giving rewarded by God?
3) Does God need money, or is there a greater purpose?
4) What helps you give lavishly to others?

Deeper Study:

2 Corinthians 9:6-15. If you sow generously, you will reap generously.

Proverbs 28:19-27. Hard work and generosity to the poor please God.

Malachi 3:7-12. Blessings await the person who gives to the Lord—don't rob Him.

Matthew 6:1-24. Don't draw attention to your giving; store up treasures in heaven.

Luke 21:1-4. Sacrificially give with a cheerful heart—it will be rewarded.

Prayer:

God, You know how often we are selfish. Forgive me, when I am stingy. I want to see the needs around me and make a difference. Thank You for challenging me to be generous. Please help me to be radical in my giving and wise in my spending. I know You will guide me, and I pray this in Jesus' name. Amen.

30) YOUR FAITH AND YOUR WORKPLACE

Passage: Ephesians 6:7-8

Serve wholeheartedly, as if you were serving the Lord, not men, because you know that the Lord will reward everyone for whatever good he does...

Insight:

It was a small job, involving some interior work at a house. A repairman, known as a Christian, was hired to complete the work, but left a huge mess for the owner to clean afterwards. A friend of the owner happened to come by his house because he was looking for a repairman to tackle an enormous project. The friend asked the owner if there was anyone he would recommend for the job. The owner, knowing the state of his house after the repairman left, simply said, "No". The repairman never knew that he just lost a very well-paying job because he was sloppy in how he finished his work. This true story is a reminder of how important it is that we not only have a good work ethic but also show respect to our employer. Our faith and our relationships are also linked to our labor.

How are your relationships in the places that you work and serve? Your labor during the day is your opportunity to display your faith. If you serve but don't have an official position, know that what you do is very significant. If you have a job, thank God for it! The way you handle yourself as you work is an extension of your worship to God. The apostle Paul lays out a clear challenge in this passage: when you work, do it all unto the Lord not merely for a person or a company. Your standard and motivation is to please God and this perspective radically changes your effort. One of the oldest tricks is to work hard only when your employer is watching. But God wants you to work with excellence at all times. Your work ethic can bring Him glory, and He isn't going to forget to reward you in His time.

Application:

Here are five things to keep in mind as you work:

1) **Unless it is sinful, do what you are hired to do with excellence.** If you want to be paid more in the future, do more than what you are asked to do now.

2) **When you see disrespect, poisonous attitudes, and rebellion on the job—don't join it.** If there is a crime or a damaging situation, you might need to report it. Overall, every job has its challenges, but keep your distance from these traps (Ecclesiastes 7:21 and Psalm 15:2-5).

3) **Your worship to God includes your special assignment from Him.** Christians don't just have jobs; they have a ministry through their work and are placed there by God for a purpose (1 Corinthians 11:1).

4) **If you are a workaholic, it's time to be honest about your reasons.** Sadly, some people indulge in work to avoid relationships at home, or derive their sense of worth by working. Some people also think God will only love them if they are always working.

5) **God's rewards are good.** Your responsibilities in heaven will be based on your faithfulness on earth. There is a reason why God often mentions rewards in the Scripture. It's because He wants you to know that He notices what you do whether you are the boss or the employee (Ephesians 6:9 and Proverbs 20:28).

Questions:

1) Who is your ultimate boss?
2) Will you make the right choice at work even if it's unpopular?
3) Are you leading by example?
4) Are you dependable and kind to everyone at your job?

Deeper Study:

Colossians 3:22-25. Work with all of your heart because you are serving God.

Proverbs 22:29. Develop your skills and God will open doors for you.

Thessalonians 3:7-13. If you are able to work, God wants you to work.

Proverbs 27:18. Respect your employer and be a blessing to your boss.

Ecclesiastes 2:24-25. A job is a gift from God- enjoy what is good about it.

Prayer:

Father God, help me to see Your purpose in my work- that it truly is a ministry. I want to do my job with excellence, love my co-workers, and represent You with my words and attitude. I pray that You will build my character, grant me strength, and provide work for me. I want to bring You glory and use the money I make to honor You. In Jesus' name I pray. Amen.

SUSTAINING GRACE

God empowers us with hope

31) THE VALUE OF ENDURANCE

Passage: 2 Corinthians 6:4-6

> *...In troubles, hardships and distresses; in beatings, imprisonments and riots; in hard work, sleepless nights and hunger; in purity, understanding, patience and kindness; in the Holy Spirit and in sincere love.*

Insight:

Because our college soccer season was in the Fall, Summer was the time to focus on conditioning. I'll admit that I often lost sleep anticipating the fitness tests that would be administered during pre-season. As a goalkeeper, I preferred to dive and make saves, not to do sprinting workouts on the track. At the beginning of the season, practices didn't involve playing soccer (it was never a good sign when we showed up for practice and our coach didn't have any soccer balls). Exercise bicycles set at full resistance, treadmills set with maximum incline to test endurance, and running with required times were all part of the training. I was thrilled to just finish in the middle of the pack. Not to be overly graphic, but I remember throwing up and then continuing the workouts. Pre-season was definitely not that enjoyable, but the results it produced were of great benefit. Have you ever extended yourself in a rigorous exercise program? If yes, how did it feel? Similar to athletic training, God can increase our capacity to endure trials in life. Jesus had joy in His sufferings because He knew the end result was worth the agony. Our character is usually refined far more in discomfort than in comfort!

What are some of the ways that God helps you and shows you grace during challenges? The apostle Paul was devoted to God but that didn't mean he faced fewer obstacles. What kind of trial didn't Paul face as he served God? As you read the book of 2 Corinthians, Paul is very open about his struggles. Each of these painful experiences proved to be a test for his steadfast decision to continue following God. Like the expanding stamina of an athlete in training, God grants you additional endurance through His constant love, encouragement, and presence. Look back through your life, what seemed impossible was accomplished through the strong, sustaining hand of God.

Application:

Read 2 Corinthians chapter 6 and learn about healthy endurance that can bring you through the darkest times:

1) **True endurance resists shady shortcuts.** When things aren't easy, you may be tempted to lie, skip important steps, or take advantage of someone. Don't compromise with something that will hurt you and diminish God's glory in your life.

2) **God gives us unique endurance for the different seasons of life.** Each year of your life is different, but God provides for each stage and every set of new challenges.

3) **Endurance is often connected with God's redemptive purposes.** It is often through trials that God will refine your character, rescue you, help you grow a deeper faith, redirect you, or display His power through you.

4) **Healthy endurance catches the eye of a watching world.** How do Christians handle adversity? Your

reactions and decisions can encourage people in incredible ways and point them to Jesus.

5) **Don't let pain close your heart to your blessings.** Pain can try to isolate you from people who can help you. Instead, let other people carry some of your burdens. Stay open to God and supportive friends.

Two quotes to inspire us:

"If God sends us on strong paths, we are provided strong shoes." [10]

- Corrie Ten Boom (survivor, Nazi concentration camps)

"Endurance is not just the ability to bear a hard thing, but to turn it into glory."[11]

-William Barclay

Questions:

1) What is the most difficult thing you are enduring now?
2) What are some possible solutions and wise options?
3) What do you think God wants you to do?

Deeper Study:

Romans 5:1-5. God builds your character with His love during your suffering.

James 1:2-4. Maturity happens when we choose to stand firm in our trials.

Romans 8:26-30. God wants to make you more like Jesus.

1 Peter 1:3-9. Genuine faith is refined through fire.

Psalm 27. Wait on God's timing and don't fear the future.

2 Thessalonians 2:13-17. Jesus will personally strengthen and encourage you.

Prayer:

My God, I commit myself to You. I pray today that I will trust Your plan and Your timing in my life. Help me to handle these challenges well. I look to You, God, because I can't do this on my own. Grant me Your perseverance, Jesus, and help me not to lose heart. I want to continue to walk closely with You in spite of the pain. I ask these things in Jesus' name. Amen.

32) SURVIVING THE DRY SEASONS

Passage: 1 Kings 17:2-4

> *Then the word of the Lord came to Elijah: "Leave here, turn eastward and hide in the Kerith Ravine, east of the Jordan. You will drink from the brook, and I have ordered the ravens to feed you there."*

Insight:

If I'm honest, there are times when watching football games seems far more appealing than reading a couple of chapters from the Bible. Spending a few hours on my twitter account is more desirable than bending my knees for a few minutes to pray. How often would you rather sleep in on Sunday morning instead of going to church? I have occasionally left church after a service realizing I hadn't even entered into worship. Like the gauges in my car that let me know I'm low on gas or oil, it's wise for me to pay attention to these signs because they are indicators for me that my spiritual life is becoming dehydrated. Like a literal drought, we can experience spiritual droughts. How do we respond to these dry seasons of testing?

God sometimes gives us some unusual directions to see if we will trust and follow Him. How strange would it be to let ravens bring dinner? It was all part of God's creative delivery plan. There was a national drought and a shortage of food and water. The prophet Elijah was not sure how to make it through such discouraging circumstances. He made the right decision by turning to God and relying on Him. His actions set the example for the nation. Elijah's name means, "The Lord is my God" and that is what he demonstrated. The nation had turned to gods who claimed to have control over the rain clouds. Through Elijah, God demonstrated His merciful provision and unmatched ability. God was looking for people who would walk with faith and look to Him. It's during the dry times that we can learn to trust God and not to let negative feelings, discouragement, or temptations run our lives.

Application:

We all face dry times spiritually. Similar to Elijah, we may be surrounded by people who are turning away from God. Or sometimes we find ourselves just going through the motions. Let's take a closer look at what Elijah did during this difficult spiritual dry spell:

1) **Stay In The Word.** Elijah listened to God. It is especially important that we keep our ears open during dry times. Keep listening. And keep reading God's Word, the Bible, even if it does not appear to be influencing anything in our lives.

2) **Stay Faithful.** We need to follow God even when emotionally we feel unenthusiastic or unmotivated. Elijah went to the Kerith Ravine simply because he was told to go. Obedience leads to blessings.

3) **Stay Calm.** We all have times that are dry spiritually; it is normal. Don't panic. God has not forgotten about us. Like Elijah, rest in this truth.

4) **Stay Open.** Elijah was willing to be fed by ravens. God might have an unusual way of providing for us. Don't ignore His small blessings and His unlikely sources. If there is something in our lives He wants to change, stay open to that too.

Questions:

1) How much of your faith is based on emotions?

2) What is true about God even when we don't feel it?

3) What do you usually do when your spiritual life is going through a dry spell?

4) Which of the four application points is most helpful for you?

5) Do you have a friend that helps to encourage you spiritually?

Deeper Study:

1 Kings 17:1-24. God has unlimited, creative ways He can provide for you.

Psalm 143. Choosing to submit to God is a key to your recovery.

1 Kings 19:1-18. God pulls us out of being self-centered and fearful.

Ezekiel 37:1-14. The real source of spiritual vitality is God; the Holy Spirit gives life.

2 Timothy 1:16-18. God can bring someone into your life that refreshes your faith.

Prayer:

Almighty God, You know how much I need You. On my own, I can get caught up just following my feelings and being overwhelmed by my circumstances. Please help me to think clearly and make good decisions. Thank You that You always care about me and you can provide in any spiritual drought. I want to stay receptive to Your solutions, directions, and promptings. I give You the glory in Jesus' name. Amen.

33) Handling Negativity

Passage: Mark 10:47-48

When he [Bartimaeus] heard that it was Jesus of Nazareth, he began to shout, "Jesus, Son of David, have mercy on me!" Many rebuked him and told him to be quiet, but he shouted all the more, "Son of David, have mercy on me!"

Insight:

It has been said that if you hang out in a barber shop long enough, you will end up getting a haircut (unless you are already bald, like me). The idea is that you tend to become very similar to the people with whom you spend the most time. The Bible warns that bad company corrupts good character (1 Corinthians 15:33). On the other hand, if you walk with the wise, you will gain wisdom (Proverbs 13:20). The Holy Spirit in you can empower you to break free from outside pressures that undermine your faith. Cry out to God stridently when the negative voices are the loudest. God's grace can silence cruel critics.

Bartimaeus was a blind beggar in the city of Jericho. No one was able to heal him. As Jesus walked by, Bartimaeus knew this was his opportunity to ask for help. He shouted once to Jesus, but the crowd told him to be quiet. Then, Bartimaeus made the most important decision of his life. He chose not to listen to the crowd. Instead, he called out to Jesus even louder the second time. Jesus saw his faith and healed him. Bartimaeus' longing for Jesus and His healing helped him prevail against the negative pressure of the crowd. The people tried to discourage him, but Bartimaeus knew that he must have faith and not give up seeking Jesus. His determination to experience the grace of Jesus helped him to overcome the peer pressure that he faced! Have you ever had to overcome people who have tried to keep you from moving forward? And rising above negativity is one of the clearest demonstrations of how the goodness of God can sustain us in any situation.

Application:

The Bible says to be careful and wise about choosing your friends (Proverbs 12:26 and 22:24). Here are some helps to manage negative pressure:

1) **Distance:** Don't get too close to people who pull you down.
2) **Double Check:** See if the Bible agrees with what you are being told by people.
3) **Reversal:** Use the negative comments to motivate you to do what is right.
4) **Firmness:** People give you advice, but you make the final decision on what to do.
5) **Avoid:** Don't step into places and situations that you can't handle.

Questions:

1) Why do people put negative pressure on themselves?
2) Are there people in your life who are pulling you away from God?
3) When have you triumphed over negative peer pressure?
4) How does the example of Bartimaeus encourage you?

Deeper Study:

Psalm 1. God's Word will help you to avoid a lot of unnecessary headaches in life.

Proverbs 13:20. You will probably become like your friends—so be discerning when choosing them.

1 Corinthians 15:33. Your character is partly shaped by other people.

Matthew 16:21-23. Well-intentioned people can lead you astray.

Philippians 2:14-16. God wants you to shine and stand out in your generation.

Galatians 2:20. Know your true identity and live out your faith.

Prayer:

Father God, I don't want to be swayed by peoples' comments and opinions. I want to be firm in my faith. Please help me not to give in to the negative influences around me. I look to Your wisdom in choosing my closest friends. I admit that I often try to please the people around me. I pray for courage and discernment so I will know when to hold my ground and when to speak up about my faith. I know You hear me now as I call out to You. I pray all of this in Jesus' name. Amen.

34)   GOD'S HELP AT JUST THE RIGHT TIME

Passage: Psalm 46:1-2

God is our refuge and strength, an ever-present help in trouble. Therefore we will not fear, though the earth give way and the mountains fall into the heart of the sea.

Insight:

I began to pray every day that I could make it through graduate school with no debt. The numbers were not in my favor. I had less than a thousand dollars when I began school, and it would cost over sixty thousand dollars to get my degree. God provided in many incredible ways. I had a tight budget, no car, and no phone at times. Beyond practical measures though, God provided. At one point, there was a man in Oakland, California, who didn't go to my church, but sensed through prayer that he was supposed to give a gift of several thousand dollars to a seminary student. My pastor called me up and told me that some unknown man in town just stopped by the church with a huge gift for a seminary student! I was the only seminary student in the church. It was just enough to pay my bills that month. Have you seen God provide for you in ways that are tremendously encouraging? And yes, God made a way so that my daily prayer was answered and I graduated with no debt. Another example of the sustaining grace of God!

As we study the timing of God in how He sustains us, there are two concepts for "time" in the Greek language. One sense of time, *chronos*, is linear; for example, there are seven days in a week. Another aspect of time is *kairos,* meaning a significant God-ordained moment. God brings *kairos* at critical junctions in our lives. The grace of God will arrive in your life with His sense of timing. God knows what we need and when we need it. Psalm 46 both acknowledges the trial that is experienced, and at the same time, gives tremendous hope. The very real presence of God and His ability to comfort and provide give the psalmist the courage to sing and praise God through difficulties. God is the source of blessing and strength, and God shows up in our darkest hours with incredible love and deliverance. It is in God's grace that we find *kairos*.

Application:

Let's take a look at how God has provided help at the right time for people:

1) **Moses:** Exodus 14:19-25. When the Israelites were trapped between the Red Sea and the army of Egypt. God demonstrated His protection and His power. He used Moses to lead the people through the parted sea into safety.

2) **Esther:** Esther 4:12-17. When the Jewish people were threatened with death, God raised up a woman named Esther and gave her a position of influence. She interceded on behalf of the Israelites and was successful in pleading with the king for their protection.

3) **Paul:** Acts 16:6-10 and 18:9-11. On Paul's journey, he didn't know what God wanted him to do. But God used a vision of a man in Macedonia to direct his steps. And when Paul was overwhelmed, Jesus appeared to Paul with comforting reassurance.

Questions:

1) Has God ever rescued you from a bleak situation?
2) How can you trust God's timing more?
3) Have you ever had an incredible answer to one of your prayers?

Deeper Study:

Zechariah 4:6-9. We need God's Spirit because our own strength is not sufficient.

Psalm 86. God hears our cries and responds when we call on Him.

Galatians 4:4-7. God knew just the right time to send His Son Jesus.

1 Chronicles 17:16-20. Humbly thank God for how He has helped you.

Prayer:

Gracious God, I need You. I'm facing situations that I can't fix or handle on my own. I thank You that You are always there. I am so grateful for Your outstanding help. Please have mercy on me and provide at this time. I will be careful to give You the glory. In Jesus' name I pray. Amen.

35)   RESPONDING WHEN TEMPTATION STRIKES

Passage: 1 Corinthians 10:13

> *No temptation has seized you except what is common to man. And God is faithful; he will not let you be tempted beyond what you can bear. But when you are tempted, he will also provide a way out so that you can stand up under it.*

Insight:

There was an old toaster in our dormitory kitchen that caused problems. Regardless of the setting, it burned the bread and the smoke would set off the fire alarm for the entire building. This happened twice in one semester, including the time when the entire dormitory was evacuated (this was after midnight, and yes it was my toast). Instead of dealing with the issue of the broken toaster, we continued to use it. Are you seeing any parallels with handling temptation?

As a pastor, I've had many people tell me that they have struggled to avoid viewing internet pornography and are not sure how to handle this temptation. What are the underlying reasons why pornography is addicting for some people? Is there any way out? Across the nation, there is heartache in many marriages as a result of this danger.

Deciding to have an extramarital affair is another destructive choice that is unfortunately eroding many marriages. What does the Bible say about resisting? There is a key principle when it comes to sexual temptation—Run! Don't go near it. Don't try to see how much you can handle. Don't come up with excuses, just quickly run away from it. When it comes to sexual temptations, it is best to avoid them altogether.

Choosing purity might mean that you take a radical step like getting rid of your computer. Or it could mean that you only use the computer when other people are in the room. Some people have decided to only use their computer during the day as the temptation usually happens late at night. You might need to distance yourself from someone who is a potential threat to your marriage. The solution might involve accountability and some limits. Avoiding the situations that are most tempting to you is a wise first step. For some people, counseling and support groups can be extremely helpful in overcoming addictions.

Do you know that God exhibits His incredible sustaining power by promising you a way out of every temptation? When I read this verse, it reminds me that God is incredibly faithful and gracious! I picture a huge exit sign and God is pointing towards it. With His help, you can truly escape any temptation. What does the way out usually look like in your everyday life?

Application:

What else helps when you are in the heat of the temptation?

1) **Prayer:** In Matthew 6:13 Jesus says that we should ask God to help lead us away from temptation and to deliver us from the evil one and his traps.

2) **Use The Word:** In Matthew chapter 4, Jesus is tempted three times. Each time He is tempted, he quotes a Bible verse. He is doing this to show us that the Word of God is powerful. Read Ephesians chapter 6. Here we learn the Bible is a weapon we can use to fight off temptations and lies.

3) **Good Decisions:** With all of our heart, begin to seek God. James tells us that if we resist the devil, he will flee from us. Set boundaries. And if we draw near to God, He will draw near to us (James 4:7-8).

It is not wrong to be tempted. Temptation is the enticement. Even Jesus was tempted. But when we are tempted, God has given us a way out, so that we can be free from it. We don't have to be locked in an unhealthy, sinful pattern. God has power for us to break out of it. God wants us to use His gracious exit when we are tempted.

Questions:

1) What intense temptations are you facing?
2) What does 1 Corinthians 10:13 say about your situation?
3) What have you learned about handling temptation?
4) How will you start using God's power to overcome these traps?

Deeper Study:

Ephesians 6:10-20. You can prevail in the spiritual battles— God empowers you.

Psalm 119:9-11. Purity is a realistic option: choose God's best for your life.

Matthew 4:1-11. Jesus quoted Bible verses when He was tempted; it works.

Prayer:

Merciful God, thank You that You are always with me even when I am tempted by this world. I know You never tempt me, but instead You help me out of trouble. I want to apply Your Word and use it to overcome the attraction of sin. I know You always give me a way out with every temptation. Please help me to take You up on Your offer and resist what is wrong. I pray this in Jesus' name. Amen.

36)   LEARNING TO PRAY

Passage: Psalm 62:8

Trust in him at all times, O people; Pour out your hearts to him, for God is our refuge.

Insight:

Psalm 62 changed the way I pray. It's a gracious invitation to go deeper into prayer with God, and He knows how much we need that communion in our relationship with Him. We derive strength from connecting with God. I remember the first time I prayed out loud: it was with a friend in his dorm room at college. It was an exciting start to prayer; I was astounded that God heard us. That night, I was walking around campus almost giddy, thinking to myself, "We just talked with God!" Without realizing it, in the next couple of years I began to settle into a pattern of prayer that over-focused on my intellectual or theological thoughts. And when I prayed with other people, that habit only intensified. It felt more like performance than authentic prayer. There were times that I was trying so hard to be correct in my wording that my soul got squeezed out of this time spent with God. Can you relate? Communication without much heart isn't what God had in mind when He created prayer. Reverence is good but so is honesty.

Psalm 62 encourages us to pour out our hearts to God. We don't need to put pressure on ourselves to have just the right words when we pray. We don't have to try to impress God with how much theology we know. He wants us to simply be ourselves and to share our lives with Him. We find great comfort in God as we pray. The Bible tells us we can approach His throne of grace with confidence (Hebrews 4:14-16) because of Jesus, and God will help us with mercy in our time of need. Know that Jesus intercedes for us in prayer, and the Holy Spirit also helps guide our communication and prayers with Father God!

Application:

When we begin to really cry out to God in prayer, sometimes it can take a long time before we see the answer to our prayers. Sometimes God does say 'no' with some of our prayer requests, because He knows when to shut the door for our own good. Sometimes we receive a "no", and it is mysterious why the door will never open. Those times can be extremely painful and disappointing.

Hannah is someone who understood about praying and not giving up. Year after year she would pray for a child. She would ask God and cry out to Him, not holding back (1 Samuel 1:1-20). Finally, God gave her a son and she named him Samuel. Samuel's name means, 'asked of the Lord'. It was because she kept asking God that God blessed her with a son.

Sometimes He responds with "not yet"; He wants us to keep praying. Jesus knows that it's easy for us to give up and stop praying, so He would often encourage His followers to keep praying. He says to keep asking, seeking, and knocking (Matthew 7:7-8). Those words encourage us to be persistent in our prayers. In Luke 18:1-8 Jesus tells a parable about how an unjust judge responds to perseverance, because Jesus wanted to point out that God who is just, will respond even more to our perseverance in prayer. Waiting is active.

There are many blessings that God is just waiting for us to ask Him for because He will grant our request. James 4:2 says, "You do not have, because you do not ask God." This is a reminder that prayer is God's chosen way of hearing us and a way that we can humble ourselves before God. When we pray, we know that it is God at work and we can't take any credit.

An Example:

Read the Lord's comments and prayer in Matthew chapter 6, verses 5 through 15. The acronym "ACTS" can keep our prayers balanced well.[12] Notice these four elements of the prayer:

1) **A**doration of God
2) **C**onfession of sins
3) **T**hanksgiving to God
4) **S**upplication by asking God's help

Questions:

1) What is easiest for you to talk with God about: your fears, sins, dreams, or pain?
2) Do you need a time of confession now to get right with God?
3) What helps you to continue to pray and not give up?
4) What prayers have you seen God answer?

Deeper Study:

Luke 11:1-13. Jesus encourages us to pray with boldness and persistence.

Philippians 4:4-9. Praying to God can remove anxiety from your heart.

Romans 8:26-27. The Holy Spirit will guide you when you don't know how to pray.

James 5:13-20. God unleashes spiritual power in response to prayer.

Prayer:

Gracious God, thank You for hearing my prayers. Pease teach me how to pray and how important prayer is each day in my relationship with You. I pray that I would trust You as I pray. I want to be full of faith and perseverance in prayer. Change my responses in life so that I am quick to pray. I know You will do great things through my prayers in Jesus' name. Amen.

FUTURE GRACE

God leads us for His name's sake

37)   THE REALITY OF HEAVEN

Passage: 2 Corinthians 5:5-8

> *Now it is God who has made us for this very purpose and has given us the Spirit as a deposit, guaranteeing what is to come. Therefore we are always confident and know that as long as we are at home in the body we are away from the Lord. We live by faith, not by sight. We are confident, I say, and would prefer to be away from the body and at home with the Lord.*

Insight:

As a young boy, my first pet was a black poodle named Monty who followed me home. After we put up signs in the neighborhood, he was unclaimed. We quickly embraced our clever little dog and became very attached to him. He created many memories in our family including when he climbed onto the oven and ate a birthday cake that wasn't for him. Have any of your pets ever done something like this? I'll never forget, years later, as I watched, when a van drove down our street and collided with Monty. He survived for a few hours before the veterinarian put him to sleep. In tears, I started to realize what death meant. For both pets and people, this life is quite temporary.

Trusting God involves the past, the present, and the future. We are grateful now for what Jesus has already done, but we eagerly anticipate what He will still accomplish. In the passage of Scripture above, Paul uses the word "confident" twice because he knows that God is dependable. Currently, we live in a body that will perish, but we have a true home in heaven and will receive new eternal bodies too. Jesus promises that anyone who puts their trust in Him will be secure with their eternal destiny (John 3:16). It is not wishful thinking, but is already accomplished by God. The promise of eternal life with Jesus is not based on our performance but instead on the grace of God through the work of Jesus' death and resurrection. The Holy Spirit is in every follower of Jesus and is a foretaste of a future destiny. The Bible tells us that Jesus wept at the funeral of his friend Lazarus. At that same funeral though, Jesus told everyone that with Him, there is life after death (John chapter eleven). Future grace allows us to savor our present blessings while at the same time look ahead to what God has promised.

Application:

The Bible Describes Heaven As: (2 Corinthians 5:1-5)

1) Permanent and real.
2) A gift from God, not earned.
3) A massive improvement from life here on earth.
4) Something we anticipate because it's so good and perfect.
5) Guaranteed by the Holy Spirit through Jesus Christ.

God's Promise Of Heaven Gives Us: (2 Corinthians 5:6-10)

1) A peaceful assurance.
2) An energizing motivation.
3) A glorious focus.

Heaven Impacts Us By: (2 Corinthians 5:11-6:2)

1) Changing the way you love other people.

2) Influencing the way you view yourself.
3) Adding meaning to your daily endeavors.
4) Making you bolder than you would normally be.

A Quote:

"If I find in myself a desire which no experience in this world can satisfy, the most probable explanation is that I was made for another world... If you read history you will find that the Christians who did the most for the present world were just those who thought most of the next. It is since Christians have largely ceased to think of the other world that they have become too ineffective in this." [13] C.S. Lewis

Questions:

1) Can someone know that they will go to heaven?
2) What aspect of heaven do you look forward to the most?
3) Do you tell other people about heaven—why or why not?
4) How can you be heavenly minded yet effective on earth?

Deeper Study:

Revelation 21:1-5. God has prepared an eternal dwelling place for you.
Luke 23:39-43. God is actively inviting people to be with Him in heaven.
1 Corinthians 13:12. In heaven, we will see Jesus face to face.
2 Peter 3:11-15. Your real home is not on this earth; it is in heaven.
1 Corinthians 2:9. Heaven will be better than anything your mind can conceive.

Prayer:

Heavenly Father, I thank You for the gift of heaven. It is so much better than any words I could use to describe it. I thank You that it's real and perfect. Thank You Jesus for dying for my sins so I will be with you in heaven. Please help me to tell as many people about heaven as I possibly can. Thank You again for Your trustworthy promises about heaven. I pray in Jesus' name. Amen.

38) WAITING ON THE LORD

Passage: 1 Samuel 30:6

David was greatly distressed because the men were talking of stoning him; each one was bitter in spirit because of his sons and daughters. But David found strength in the Lord his God.

Insight:

Living in Aberdeen, Scotland, helped me appreciate the incredible tenacity and determination of the locals. Yes, I did try the haggis, (a "pudding" containing oatmeal, onion, sheep's heart, liver, and lungs) and one bite was sufficient. I thoroughly enjoyed the various accents throughout the country. There is an ongoing debate about the existence of the Loch Ness monster. One gentleman, on a television program, said that he had indeed seen the legendary beast and if he had to spend the rest of his life in the same spot just to get another glimpse of Nessie, he surely would! I really don't think he was joking. His willingness to wait for Nessie to appear definitely demonstrates commitment. In a unique way, it also makes me think I should be more excited and patient in waiting to catch a glimpse of God's fingerprints.

Waiting can be actively living out our faith. Waiting shows how we can respond to God when we haven't yet received the longings of our hearts. With pressure and stress surrounding him, David gave us an example of how to wait. He was anointed king of Israel, but he had to wait for more than 13 years to begin his new role. During that time, the reigning king, Saul, attempted to kill David several times. David was on the run and living just a step away from death for years. At one point, the men with him became frustrated and turned against David. David was all alone. But he did not give up. Instead he turned to the Lord and found strength. As it turned out, David would become the king of

Israel just a few days after this test. Even though David had been waiting for over 13 years, and the situation did not look good, he was actually on the verge of his breakthrough!

All of us choose a foundation for our future. Jesus talks about building your house on the rock so that when the rains come, the streams rise, and the winds blow against your house, it will not fall (Matthew 7:24-29). Life can feel like a constant treadmill of demands and responsibilities. The pace can be overwhelming. As we wait, it is important to stop and reflect on a deeper level and examine the motivations that underlie our daily decisions. Trusting God with our future allows us to handle our present "delays" with grace.

Application:

Waiting is not something people usually enjoy. It can be difficult sitting in the waiting rooms in the hospital. Have you ever tried to spend the night sitting in one of those chairs? Have you ever had to wait for the doctor to give you the results of a procedure when your loved one has been in the operating room for many hours? In stores, I work hard to find the shortest line (do you ever speed up to get ahead of another customer?). Honestly, I often don't even let the microwave finish cooking before I pull out my food (I'll just open up the microwave door with 3 seconds left because I don't want to wait any longer). Waiting, however, is a common experience. We wait for a class to end, we wait for the end of the school year, we wait for a best friend, we wait for sex until marriage, we wait to get a car and have our own place to live, we wait for healing from the pain we have experienced in life, we wait for Jesus to return. No matter how much we want to rush through life, there are still many circumstances when we need to wait on God! Have you ever rushed into a bad decision? Waiting can actually reveal God's wisdom and strengthen our confidence in Him and His grace.

Here are some encouraging principles to help during the waiting times:

1) **Waiting is often active**. Even though David spent over thirteen years of his life waiting to be king, he did not just sit around. He took care of sheep, he played an instrument, he made friends, he was a leader, he wrote, and he worked hard. Don't just sit around and feel sorry for yourself; ask God what He wants you to do as you wait. Don't give up.

2) **Waiting usually ends**. Even if it lasts longer than you want, most waiting is just for a season. Remember that God is still in control and God is good. He does not always reveal His purposes during the times when we wait, but He wants us to use those times to grow. Don't be discouraged.

3) **Waiting tests where you find your strength**. David learned how to find strength in The Lord. It is very important to go to church and to have friends who encourage you in your faith, but we still need to learn how to gain strength from God in our own times alone with Him. Your best tool for getting through waiting will be your connection with the living God. Praising Him alone, opening up your heart, mourning with Him, and absorbing His word and promises are all essential. You may develop a new depth in your relationship with God as you wait.

When Grace Is Missing

Not all soil is the same. The amount of nutrients, acidity, capacity to support life, and climate are significant considerations. It's the roots in life that produce the fruit. Toxic soils take over when we aren't rooted in grace, and they turn waiting into frustration:

1) **Rooted In Fear:** Evidenced by worry, timidity, and sleeplessness.

2) **Rooted In Selfishness:** Evidenced by a self-centered absorption.

3) **Rooted In Bitterness:** Evidenced by hostility, rage, revenge, and hatred.

4) **Rooted In Despair:** Evidenced by giving up and beating yourself up.

God has something much better for us than these unhealthy soils. When you understand future grace, your attitude changes as you are waiting. Jesus not only forgives our sins and gives us eternal life, but He also changes us from the inside out. As we wait on Him, God wants to pull us out of the mire and enable us to walk on the heights (Psalm 40). Future grace invites us to make clear decisions of faith today, knowing that God's way is ultimately for His glory and our good.

Questions:

1) What are the most significant things that you are waiting for now?

2) How have you handled your waiting times in the past?

3) How do you prevent becoming too passive when you are waiting?

4) What does it mean to find your strength in God and how do you do it?

Deeper Study:

1 Samuel 30:1-25. Learn how to find strength in God as you wait.

Psalm 130. God's unfailing love is your confidence; His timing is good.

Isaiah 30:15-18. The Lord longs to be gracious to you—don't resist.

Romans 8:22-27. The entire earth is longing for God's eternal redemption.

Hebrews 9:27-28. A day will come when all of your waiting is over.

Prayer:

Sovereign God, I realize that my timing is not always Your timing. Forgive me when I think I know what is best and try to call all of the shots. I want to grow in my willingness to wait on You. I know waiting can be a good thing. Help me to redeem those times of waiting by trusting You and growing in my faith. Grant me Your patience and perspective I pray in Jesus' name. Amen.

39) DISCOVERING SECURITY

Passage: 1 John 5:11-13

And this is the testimony: God has given us eternal life, and this life is in his Son. He who has the Son has life; he who does not have the Son of God does not have life. I write these things to you who believe in the name of the Son of God so that you may know that you have eternal life.

Insight:

Even before I was one year old, my life almost ended. Have you had any near-death experiences? My parents were in a canoe with me, enjoying a ride on the river. Suddenly, the canoe tipped over and they couldn't find me. After multiple dives underwater, I still couldn't be found. Too much time had elapsed, and it appeared I drowned. On a third and final dive, my mother located me trapped under the corner of the canoe and pulled me loose up to the surface of the water. I don't remember that day, but gratitude swells in my heart whenever I hear the story. God has used my mom to rescue me on a number of occasions. It makes me realize my life is a gift. God has purposes for you that start on earth and lead into eternity.

God's grace never ends. Jesus wants you to always experience His grace. God says that you will have eternal life when you put your trust in His Son, Jesus, as your Savior. These verses were written so that you will have God's promise given to you very clearly. Eternal life and the forgiveness of sins is not something you can earn; it is an undeserved gift! If it was based on your performance and morality, then your confidence would waver. But this promise is based on Jesus and the fact that He died for our sins at the cross and overcame death. This is not only the greatest pardon known to humanity; it is also an assurance that God wants you to have: you have been eternally rescued! No one can change the reality and reliability of God's promises. The gift of eternal life is free for you. But this gift cost Jesus His life and The Father His Son.

Let these verses sink in deeply. This is an aspect of future grace that many people unnecessarily resist. Since you can trust Him with heaven, know God is also faithful to you in your daily schedule and relationships. Next time stress increases, demands are overwhelming, the pace is exhausting and no relief is in sight, remember Who holds your future. Let Him give you His perspective and His plan. He is Lord of the big picture and the finer details. Serve God with gratitude, confidence in His Word, and a teachable heart.

Application:

Can anyone find ultimate security or lasting joy in these options? Not everything on this motley list is detrimental, but how do we know when something becomes a substitute for God in our lives? What are the limitations of each topic on this list? Do you ever see people pursuing these aspects of life, hoping to discover lasting contentment?

1) **Accomplishments:** Having awards, good grades, and an impressive resume.
2) **Beauty:** Looking into the mirror with the right outfit or plenty of muscles.
3) **Toughness:** Putting up walls and not admitting needs or letting people help.
4) **Popularity:** Constantly trying to impress people.
5) **Money:** Loving it and placing wealth as the highest priority.
6) **Dating:** Thinking if we find just the right person we will finally be secure.
7) **Drugs:** Hoping chemicals will bring happiness and eliminate pain.

Questions:

1) What kind of security do each of these seven options bring and for how long?
2) What is the price tag for putting our trust in these seven options?
3) Can you know that you have eternal life and acceptance from God?
4) What happens when you are secure in the deepest part of your being?

Deeper Study:

John 10:27-30. No one can snatch you out of God's hand.

1 John 4:13-18. God's Spirit lives in you forever.

Deuteronomy 33:12. You can find rest and security with God.

John 5:24-27. Putting your trust in Jesus changes your eternal destiny.

Titus 3:4-8. No one can earn their way to heaven—it is by the grace of Jesus.

Prayer:

Faithful God, all of Your promises are reliable. I receive Your word today that You give me an eternal promise because I have put my trust in Jesus. I want to believe Your word even when it seems too good to be true. There is real peace and rest deep within me because I know You love me. I am so grateful that You give me eternal life with You, and that no one can take it away. I thank You for your grace to me in Jesus' name. Amen.

40)   A DAY LIKE NO OTHER

Passage: John 14:1-3

Jesus said, "Do not let your hearts be troubled. Trust in God; trust also in me. In my Father's house are many rooms; if it were not so, I would have told you. I am going there to prepare a place for you. And if I go to prepare a place for you, I will come back and take you to be with me that you also may be where I am."

Insight:

When a day is going to be significant, there is a countdown. High school and college seniors know their graduation date even when it's over 100 days away. (Yes, I was part of that group.) Engaged couples want to run down the aisle months before their ceremony. (The month before our wedding may have been the slowest 31 days of my life.) Excited parents closely watch the calendar as they anticipate their baby's due date. (Enjoy the opportunities to sleep too!) Exhausted employees get a surge of energy as they tell you about their plans for retirement. We are wired to look forward to coming events. Longing for an improved future is a desire that will be fulfilled. There is a day on God's schedule when He will usher in a new heaven, and earth.

The promises of God are drenched in His grace! There are so many promises in the Bible that relate to our future. In this passage, Jesus states that after His death and resurrection He will go to heaven. As we wait for His return, He reminds us to not give in to despair. This world is starved for hope, but there is incredible hope when we choose to trust God. And Jesus gave us a promise with a full guarantee that He is preparing a place for us in heaven and one day He will return and take His followers to be with Him forever. Jesus' return is not a question mark; it is a fact.

Application:

What does the Bible say should be our response to His return?

1) **Don't try to guess the hour of His return.** Acts 1:6-7 tells us that we will not know the exact time of His return. It will come unannounced. Unfortunately, many people won't be ready for it. The Bible says no one will ever be able to know the exact time of Jesus' return. Ignore any "experts" who claim to have figured out the date.

2) **Long for His appearing.** 2 Timothy 4:8 confirms that it will be an incredibly good day for all of those who love Jesus. It is good to want this day to come soon.

3) **Get rid of rebellion.** 2 Peter 3:10-13 describes the intensity of that day and how we are to be prepared now by living a pure and holy life. May Jesus find us faithful when He returns.

4) **Be aware of the signs of the times.** In Matthew chapter 24, Jesus gave several warnings and prophecies about the end times. Don't be naive, pay attention to what is happening in the world.

Questions:

1) What movies and books are there about Jesus' return: are they accurate?

2) Have you studied Biblical prophecy or the book of Revelation; if yes, what did you learn?

3) What changes do you need to make in your life knowing Jesus will return?

4) What do you find most comforting about the promises of Jesus and His return?

5) What can you do to let the world know about Jesus' return?

Deeper Study:

1 Thessalonians 4:13-18. You will meet the Lord and be with Him forever.

1 Corinthians 15:12-58. You will receive a resurrected body that won't perish.

Acts 1:1-11. Jesus' return will be physical and visible; eagerly await that day.

Matthew 24:26-51. Jesus' return will be sudden and unexpected like lightning.

Revelation 22:7-21. God guarantees that Jesus will return and reign: be ready.

Prayer:

Faithful God, I know that You will keep your promises, and Jesus will return. I eagerly look forward to that day. Even if the world rejects Your truth, Your plan can't be stopped. Thank You for preparing a place for me in heaven. I confidently rest in Your guarantee today and spread the good news, in Jesus' name. Amen.

41)   MOVING FORWARD BY FAITH

Passage: Job 23:8-10

> *But if I go to the east, he is not there; If I go to the west, I do not find him. When he is at work in the north, I do not see him; when he turns to the south, I catch no glimpse of him. But he knows the way that I take; when he has tested me, I will come forth as gold.*

Insight:

How can God be omnipresent (present everywhere) and at the same time be so difficult to find? Have you ever had times when you wanted to see God and be close to Him, but it just didn't happen? That was Job's experience. In these verses, Job said that he was actively seeking out God, but the results were discouraging. In the end though, Job's desires for God were fulfilled. But clearly, the timing is God's. And for us the emptiness of the search is a reality and part of the journey. Maturity doesn't usually happen without trials, including the one described in the following story.

Application:

Gerald Sittser lost his mom, wife and daughter in a car accident. In his book, *A Grace Disguised*, Sittser writes, "Loss may call the existence of God into question. Pain seems to conceal him from us, making it hard for us to believe that there could be a God in the midst of our suffering. In our pain we are tempted to reject God...we wrestle in our souls to believe." Can you imagine that? Gerald lost three generations of the women he loved in his family in one car crash. He writes about what he has learned: "I don't think I will ever be able to comprehend God's sovereignty...I have made peace with his sovereignty and have found comfort in it. It is no longer odious to me." [14] This is an incredible perspective that Gerald shares: God doesn't abandon us, even when we can't sense Him there. This confidence in God allows Gerald to move forward in life, knowing he is not alone.

The Bible says that there are times in our lives when God just carries us (Exodus 19:4, Deuteronomy 1:31, Isaiah 40:11, and Isaiah 63:9). There are other times when we are at a crossroad in life, and God wants us to continue to walk forward in the direction He guides (Isaiah 30:21). His whisper is the reassurance our ears are longing to hear! As we choose to continue along the path with Him in spite of pain, we bring Him glory. We learn that His grace is not just for our present situation, He goes before us with grace into our future.

Questions:

1) What does it mean to live by faith?
2) How can God bring good out of bad situations?
3) How does perseverance play a role in your faith?
4) How does God use challenges to help lead us to maturity?

Deeper Study:

Matthew 5:1-12. Jesus makes it very clear what He values.

Haggai 2:1-9. Don't despise small beginnings—leave the results in God's hands.

Obadiah 1:3-4. Pride and faith don't exist together; make your selection.

Micah 6:6-8. Obedience is better than sacrifice and leads to a bright future.

Psalm 23. The Lord is your Shepherd who restores you soul.

Prayer:

God, thank You that You don't abandon me when I'm in the valley of doubt. Your hand reaches down and picks me up. You give me the ability to walk by faith and apply what I have learned. I want to approach situations with confidence in You and have the eyes to see how You are working. Order my steps in Your word. I pray in Jesus' name. Amen.

42) TOO GOOD NOT TO SHARE

Passage: John 1:40-42

Andrew, Simon Peter's brother, was one of the two who heard what John had said and who had followed Jesus. The first thing Andrew did was to find his brother Simon and tell him, "We have found the Messiah" (that is the Christ). And he brought him to Jesus...

Insight:

On the day I proposed to Laurie (I'm so blessed that she said yes), we were ecstatic. We wanted to celebrate so we drove to a romantic restaurant on the waterfront. In the parking lot before we got out of the car, we began to call people, and call, and call! After many giddy announcements of our engagement, we finally walked over to the restaurant. Much to our surprise, because we spent so long in the car talking with people, it was now closed. Without realizing it, sharing with the people we loved was far more important than the appetizing food. The locked front door just gave me another opportunity to tell someone else our story. The same waitress who told us the restaurant was closed, after hearing about our engagement, now let us in for a special exception: two desserts. Doors that were closed began to open as she wanted to give us something for our engagement. Grace is often contagious; it is more caught than taught!

When was the last time you were so excited about something that you had to tell people about it? Andrew urgently found his brother Simon because he wanted to tell him about Jesus. Underneath it all was simply a deep love for Simon and an awareness of the greatness of Jesus. Andrew had a sense that their future was about to change in a remarkable way. When you experience Jesus, His grace ignites your passion. You become connected to a purpose that spans all generations, and He invites you into a new future. As you share your journey and the pure joy of discovering who Jesus is, God will open up incredible opportunities for you. Remember that it was Andrew who told his brother Simon about Jesus. This is the same Simon who Jesus would later rename Peter, calling him a rock and a pillar in the early church. Andrew cared too much about his brother to not tell him about the Messiah! The direction of their lives was about to be transformed by the grace of Jesus.

Application:

We often talk ourselves out of sharing what is most important to us in life. Can you relate to any of these excuses?
1)   I don't know exactly how to say it.
2)   I might lose the friendship if I tell them.
3)   I'm not an extrovert.
4)   I don't have all of the answers.
5)   I have a story that isn't very interesting.

Notice that every excuse begins with the same letter "I" (not a coincidence). When we focus on our own abilities and inadequacies, we become paralyzed and silent. Andrew wasn't thinking about himself; he cared for Simon and had his thoughts on Jesus. Read Exodus chapter three and observe how God helped Moses see through his own excuses and shift his focus onto the great I AM. Mike Helton was the first person who ever told me about Jesus and I'm so grateful for him. He was scared when he talked to me and stumbled over some words, but God really showed me his love through what Mike said to me.

International Opportunities:

There is an African proverb that states, "The greatest crime in a desert is to find water and keep silent about it."[15] It has become increasingly easier to bless someone who is from a different country by sharing your faith, family, and finances. Consider these practical ways that you can make a difference when it comes to sharing your faith and spreading God's love and grace in your home and throughout the world.[16]

1) Pray for people around the world.

2) Go serve in another nation.

3) Welcome an international student into your home.

4) Give financially to support a missionary.

5) Sponsor a child (www.compassion.org)

6) Use the internet to help people grow in their faith. (www.globalmediaoutreach.com)

7) Encourage more people to be involved in what God is doing globally.

Questions:

1) Who are the people that have shared the love of Jesus with you?

2) Why is it so significant to share your faith?

3) When has God helped you to overcome some of your own excuses?

4) How can you really make an eternal difference in someone's life?

Deeper Study:

2 Kings 7:1-20. The men who had leprosy became generous and lived.

Romans 1:16-17. There is no reason to be ashamed of Jesus.

1 Peter 3:15-16. Share the facts behind your faith with gentleness.

Colossians 4:2-6. Let your conversations be always full of grace.

Acts 1:8. Jesus will use you to reach out to people all over the world.

Prayer:

Gracious God, thank You for reaching out to me. I want to be someone who extends Your love. Grant me the vision and courage to see the needs in this world. I want to look beyond my own country. You have given me the resources to make a difference and serve. I also know that it's your desire that everyone has an opportunity to hear about the love of Jesus. Guide my words so that I might know what to say. I rely on the Holy Spirit to help me. I pray this all in your name, Jesus. Amen.

Grace For The Journey

In 1992, on a flight from Boston to Zimbabwe, I anticipated there would be some layovers. However, I don't always pay attention to details and failed to notice that one of my stops would be in The Azores Islands. When we approached the islands, the breath-taking beauty of the scenery created feelings of admiration and wonder inside of me. As we landed, I was captivated beyond my expectations. Is there a place on earth that has had this kind of effect on you? Being in The Azores and experiencing the grace of God have some similarities for me: 1) I didn't know how exquisite they were until I personally tasted their goodness, 2) I couldn't arrive there on my own: one journey required an airplane, the other a Savior, 3) each experience existed to be embraced and enjoyed, 4) for each experience, I had a feeling of privilege and gratitude, 5) both ultimately pointed me to my benevolent Maker.

John Piper, in his book *Desiring God*, asks, "Do people go to the Grand Canyon to increase their self-esteem? Probably not. This is, at least, a hint that the deepest joys in life come not from savoring the self, but from seeing splendor. And in the end even the Grand Canyon will not do. We were made to enjoy God."[17] We will not be fulfilled in life when we are consumed with ourselves. Jesus boldly claims that He has come to give us abundant life (John 10:10) which includes His grace both on a daily basis and forever. It is a gift that we are wise to receive. We decide everyday if our lives will be rooted in grace.

Thomas Aquinas concluded that the splendor of a soul in grace is so seductive that it surpasses the beauty of all created things.[18] My hope is that God will drench you with His grace in meaningful and practical ways. In the words of the apostle Paul, "...And I pray that you, being rooted and established in love, may have power, together with all the saints, to grasp how wide and long and high and deep is the love of Christ, and to know this love that surpasses knowledge—that you may be filled to the measure of all the fullness of God (Ephesians 3:17-19)." As your journey continues, how much of the grace of Jesus do you want in your life? Jesus is abounding in love and is completely dependable. Not only can Jesus sustain, heal, and empower you, but profound joy comes when you see His grace flood the hearts of people you love.

Notes

1. McDowell, Josh. *Evidence That Demands A Verdict.* Nashville, TN: Thomas Nelson, 1999.

2. Goldsmith, Donald. *The Astronomers.* New York, NY: St. Martin's Press, 1991: 39.

3. Smith, Timothy. *The Faith of Johann Sebastian Bach.* Riemenschneider Bach Institute, published in the BACH Journal 28:1-2 (Spring-Summer/Fall-Winter 1997).

4. *The Donnie McClurkin Story: From Darkness To Light.* Dir. Stephanie A. Frederic. Image Entertainment. 2004. DVD.

5. *One Life.* Dir. Joyce Meyer. Joyce Meyer Ministries. n.d. DVD.

6. Meyer, Joyce. *Beauty For Ashes: Receiving Emotional Healing.* Fenton, MI: Warner Books, 2004.

7. Orr, J. Edwin. *The Light of The Nations.* London, England: PaterNoster Press, 1965.

8. Lewis, CS. *Mere Christianity.* San Francisco, CA: Harper Collins, 2001.

9. "About Us." *Compassion International®.* n.p. n.d. Web. 18 Jan. 2012.

10. ThinkExist.com Quotations. "Corrie Ten Boom quotes." *ThinkExist.com Quotations Online.* 1 Dec. 2011. Web. 18 Jan. 2012.

11. "William Barclay." *BrainyQuote.com. Xplore Inc.* 2012. Web. 18 Jan. 2012.

12. Hybels, Bill. *Too Busy Not To Pray.* Downers Grove, IL: InterVarsity Press, 1998.

13. Lewis, CS. *Mere Christianity.* San Francisco, CA: Harper Collins, 2001.

14. Sittser, Jerry. *A Grace Disguise*d. Grand Rapids, MI: Zondervan, 2004

15. "Famous African Proverbs." *Special Dictionary.* n.p. 2012. Web. 18 Jan. 2012.

16. Ahrend, Todd. "World Christian Habits." *The Traveling Team.* n.p. n.d. Web. 18 Jan. 2012.

17. Piper, John. *Desiring God.* Colorado Springs, CO: Multnomah Books, 2003.

18. Manning, Brennan. *The Ragamuffin Gospel.* Sisters, OR: Multnomah Books, 2005: 93.

Bibliography

Walvoord and Zuck. *The Bible Knowledge Commentary: New Testament Edition*. Colorado Springs, CO: Victor Books, 1983.

Walvoord and Zuck. *The Bible Knowledge Commentary: Old Testament Edition*. Colorado Springs, CO: Victor Books, 1985.

Pfeiffer and Harrison. *The Wycliffe Bible Commentary*. Chicago, IL: Moody Press, 1990.

Gaebelein, Barker, etc. *The Expositor's Bible Commentary*. Grand Rapids, MI: Zondervan, 1992.